TEAMS ARE ADAPTIVE SYSTEMS:
12 PRINCIPLES FOR EFFECTIVE MANAGEMENT

Luca Dellanna
@DellAnnaLuca
Luca-dellanna.com

First edition
January 2021

Luca Dell'Anna © 2021 – All Rights Reserved

[Page intentionally left blank]

Other books by Luca Dellanna:

Best Practices for Operational Excellence, Second Edition (2020)

Ergodicity: Definition, Examples, And Implications (2020)

The Control Heuristic, Second Edition (2020)

100 Truths You Will Learn Too Late (2019)

The Power of Adaptation (2018)

The World Through a Magnifying Glass (2018)

TABLE OF CONTENTS

Introduction 5

Chapter 1 **Teams are adaptive systems** 7

Chapter 2 **Avoid motivational losses** 18

Chapter 3 **Surface problems** 32

Chapter 4 **Give specific feedback** 44

Chapter 5 **Systematically remove grey areas** 58

Chapter 6 **Lead by example with costly signaling** 68

Chapter 7 **Work on the root causes first** 79

Chapter 8 **Use tight feedback loops** 89

Chapter 9 **Go where the work takes place** 98

Chapter 10 **Take decisions not just for their result but for how they affect future behavior** 114

Chapter 11 **You are an adaptive system too** 121

Chapter 12 **Change is achieved one focus at a time** 127

Tying it all together 132

Aftermath 134

About the Author 135

Other books by Luca Dellanna 136

    Acknowledgments 145

INTRODUCTION

Welcome to "Teams Are Adaptive Systems: 12 Principles For Effective Management."

I have been working in Operational Excellence for almost nine years and observed or consulted hundreds of companies.

From experience, I can tell you that the most important and most neglected managerial concept is that teams are adaptive systems. **Motivation, skills, and performance are not static traits of their team members. Instead, they are the reactions to the actions of the manager. Not to his words, not to his promises, but to his actions.**

Hence why I decided to write this book. Twelve principles that describe the ripples that your actions will have on the motivation, skills, and performance of your team.

COMPASSES, NOT MAPS

Maps are great to orientate yourself, as long as the territory doesn't change. A map of Chicago is hardly useful if you are in New York, and even a map of the correct city can get outdated fast. For this reason, in this book, I will not tell you many stories of what a great executive did. What worked for him in his company at the time might not work for you, in your company, today.

Instead, I will give you 12 principles that are like compasses. Timeless, useful, and precise, no matter where you are and where you're going.

DO WHAT WORKS

The content of this book describes and leverages the team dynamics that I observed being common in the many companies I had a chance to observe. Your organization might or might not be different.

If something works for you and your team, keep doing it. You know your organization better than any outsider, including me. Just make sure that it works for you *and* for your team *and* for your organization – not just one or two of the three – and that it works in the short *and in* the long term. This book will help you assess this.

For any question, feel free to email me at **Luca@Luca-Dellanna.com**

On to the First Principle!

DISCLAIMER

Always use common sense. Nothing in this book is financial advice or advice of any other kind. The author shall not be held liable for the application or misapplication of the contents of this book. You can find a link to my full disclaimer at **Luca-dellanna.com**

CHAPTER 1
TEAMS ARE ADAPTIVE SYSTEMS

The human species is incredible. We explored seas, mountains, and space. We adapted to live in cities and to work jobs that didn't exist. We humans have an unrivaled capacity for adaptation.

That very capacity for adaptation also applies to employees at the workplace. A new hire with a demanding yet fair boss adapts to grow his skills and his ambition. One with a boss that demands but never gives will pivot his contribution from performance to excuses.

The single most useful lens to observe and understand workplace behavior is that **teams are adaptive systems. Their components – employees – adapt to their work environment and, in particular, to his or her manager's actions.**

For example, **motivation is an adaptation to a work environment in which results bring positive outcomes.** If completing a task brings us a reward or a feeling of accomplishment or respect, it is only natural to want to do more of it. If you, as a manager, reward an employee of yours for a good result he brought, even just with a sincere thank you, I guarantee that he will get motivated.

REWARD RESULTS, NOT EFFORTS

Of course, you need to make sure that you reward results, not efforts. Otherwise, your employees will adapt by bringing fewer results and showing more effort.

Conversely, if an employee of yours obtains a good result and you fail to reward him – again, even just with a nod of the head –, you give him a work environment in which results go unrewarded. It is only rational for him to adapt by decreasing his engagement.

MOTIVATION IS AN ADAPTATION

Indeed, **motivation is not a personal trait set in stone. It is an adaptation to an event that reveals that the benefits of an action were worth its costs.**

Employees whose results are acknowledged grow motivated.

More importantly, employees whose results pass unobserved quickly grow demotivated. Their days at the workplace become a collection of clues that efforts are not worth it. **The rational adaptation for them is to minimize efforts.**

> Motivation is an adaptation.
> It is a reaction to events revealing that efforts are worth it.
>
> A lack of motivation is an adaptation too.
> It is a reaction to events revealing that efforts are not worth it.

INTERNAL AND EXTERNAL MOTIVATION ARE BOTH FORMS OF ADAPTATION

Some employees are externally motivated. Their motivation (or lack thereof) is an adaptation to an environment in which individual consequences follow (or do not follow) results.

Other employees appear to be internally motivated. Even in their case, motivation is an adaptation to cues that efforts are worth it. The difference is that they create these clues themselves. For example, they might grab pleasure or self-respect from learning new skills or from seeing themselves having done a good job.

Few employees are internally motivated. Most need the environment to provide them with clues that their efforts won't go to waste. You, as a manager, can help create such an environment.

Two factors are needed for an environment to provide clues that employees' efforts are not wasted. One, the employees must be able to convert their efforts into results. They might need skills to do that. If these are absent, you need to train them. **Two, the environment must provide rewards for their results.** You, as a manager, can set this environment or provide these rewards. For example, there are best practices you can use to ensure that you can catch the good results of your employees and reward them with a thank you – they'll be the object of a later chapter.

EVERYTHING IS AN ADAPTATION

If you acknowledge that teams are adaptive systems, it follows that at least some of the traits that you observe in your employees are rational adaptations to the events they went through.

These past experiences might have taken place at their current workplace, at a previous one, at school, or at home. Very often, the emotional baggage people carry is an adaptation to events of their past. Trauma is an adaptation. An overadaptation, perhaps, but an adaptation nevertheless. Laziness is an adaptation. Passivity is an adaptation. And so on. You cannot do anything to change the past of your employees, but you can help them find clues that they are in a different environment now.

Whatever workplace environment you give to your employees, they will adapt to it. Of course, there are some individual traits and circumstances over which you have no control. However, whether you give them an environment in which results are rewarded or ignored is largely in your control.

MOTIVATION IS AN ADAPTATION TO EMOTIONAL REWARDS

I have used the word "rewards" a few times so far. With it, I do not only intend formal rewards such as bonuses, promotions, or letters of merit. These are necessary to recognize sustained performance over time – no matter what else you do, an outstanding employee whose performance is not formally recognized is likely to leave your organization at some point – but they are not enough.

You can hardly award formal rewards more than once a year. This makes them unfit for adaptation purposes. Employees expect you to recognize their good immediately, not at the end of the year. If an employee makes a great contribution in, say, February, he expects you to thank him for it in February, not later. By December, he will already have adapted to a lack of rewards.

Hence the necessity to use informal rewards, such as thank yous, handshakes, and other forms of acknowledgment that say, "good job." These are the only ones that you can apply fast enough to consistently prevent a feeling of "my good results are not appreciated here" and the consequent rational adaptation to minimize one's efforts.

> **Informal rewards provide the necessary immediacy**
> to avoid seeing one's efforts go unrewarded

Before describing in better detail how the rewards you give and do not give trigger adaptations, let me repeat a very important point. **People need both formal and informal rewards.** We need formal ones because money and status are a big part of why people work – and even if we don't need the money, we don't want to feel underpaid. Moreover, we need informal rewards because we all want to know that our efforts were not wasted, and we want to know it immediately.

This last part about immediacy is not a choice or a whim, but the consequence of the way our brain is wired. Whenever we take action, our brain produces an expectation of an emotional reward. If we get the reward, chemical changes take place that reinforce the behavior. They make us desire to repeat it, eventually making it a habit. If we do not get the reward, or if we get it too late, other chemical changes take place that make us less likely to repeat the behavior in the future.

To sustain performance, employees need frequent informal rewards

This is the consequence our brain is wired. Performance followed by a lack of reward leads to demotivation.

Informal rewards are anything that creates a feeling of happiness, relief, progress, self-confidence, or self-respect. They can be "thank yous", "good jobs!", signs of respect like higher autonomy, being acknowledged as the "go-to guys" for some narrow topic, the chance to work on prestige projects, handshakes, nods of approval, and so on.

There is some individual difference in how people respond to different kinds of rewards. It is part of your job as a manager to get to know your team and figure out how to dispense the most appropriate and effective informal rewards. As a rule of thumb, begin with a sincere "good job!"

INAPPROPRIATE REWARDS

Here is a common mistake that managers make after learning that employees need frequent rewards to sustain high performance.

Instead of learning the lesson that "to avoid motivational losses, you should reward good performance," some managers learn the wrong lesson that "rewards generate good performance." They then begin saying "good job" to everyone, no matter whether these employees did anything to deserve it. The resulting environment is "my manager tells me good job no matter what I do." The consequent adaptation is "the optimal level of effort is no effort."

Instead, good managers understand that they should only reward performance worth being rewarded. Rewarding anything else leads to complacence, mistrust, or to the rest of the team being upset for the unfair treatment.

Moreover, good managers also understand that they do not have to wait for quarterly results or year-end evaluations to reward performance. Instead, good managers look at opportunities to catch their employees doing "a tiny bit of great performance." Then, they tell him, "good job *for that*." That allows for faster feedback.

For example, John's manager does not wait for John's quarterly numbers to tell him how he feels about his performance. Instead, whenever he passes by John, he observes what he is doing or asks him updates on the projects he is working on. He makes sure to do it in a friendly and non-inquisitive way. As soon as he catches a genuine reason to tell John "good job," he does so. These reasons are usually instances of desirable behavior. If John visited an important client in person instead of sending an email, and that is a behavior that John's manager wants to see more often, then he should tell John "good job."

At all times, you should look for opportunities to give your employees the environment that makes sustainable performance the rational adaptation.

Frequent informal rewards following desired behaviors are one of the best ways to do that.

There are other options, but they are worse. For example, "sticks and carrots" have a high risk of leading to minimum compliance (employees do just enough to avoid the stick or get the carrot and nothing more than that) and side effects (employees try to "game the system" to avoid the stick or get the carrot without doing the work that was intended).

Instead, **frequent informal rewards have the frequency and specificity to ensure that they only reward the desired behavior** so that the resulting adaptation is beneficial for the organization.

> **Sticks and carrots (alone) generate unintended consequences**
>
> such as lack of performance beyond the minimum needed or at anything except what is being measured.

A further chapter will describe more in detail the various types and ways in which you can reward your employees. For the moment, let's see a general lens you can use to guide your managerial actions.

THE ADAPTATION LENS

The lens you should use at all times is the following.

With my actions, what environment am I creating for my team, and what adaptations will it trigger?

If you acquire the habit of asking yourself this question often, you will understand much better the long-term impact of your actions on the performance of your team.

FAIRNESS

At all times, you should strive to be fair. This is not only a good moral compass. It is also useful to avoid most unintended consequences in your managerial actions. Here are some examples:
- Failing to reward an employee's good performance is unfair *and* leads to him getting demotivated.
- Rewarding an employee's mediocre performance is unfair to his better-performing teammate *and* leads to the team losing motivation.
- Rewarding a mediocre employee for a single instance of good performance is fair *and* leads to him gaining motivation.
- Failing to tell an employee that his performance was subpar is unfair *and* leads to him learning that mediocrity is okay or that excellence is unrewarded.

These were just a few examples. This book will cover more in further chapters. By the end of it, you will have learned that fairness is one of the most useful compasses to guide your actions from a team management perspective.

> **A fair work environment is the most motivating,**
> and an unfair one, the most demotivating.

A SUMMARY OF THIS CHAPTER

- Employees adapt to their work environment.

- In particular, motivation is a rational adaptation to a fair environment in which results are rewarded. (And a lack of motivation is a rational adaptation to an unfair environment in which results are wastes of effort.)

- Frequent informal rewards should complement formal rewards. The immediacy of the former is necessary to prevent a feeling of "my good results are not appreciated here" and the consequent rational adaptation to minimize one's efforts.

- At all moments, strive to be fair. It is motivating, and it prevents your managerial actions from creating unintended side-effects.

- The adaptation lens: "with my actions, which environment am I creating for my team, and what adaptations will it trigger?"

EXERCISES

1) Think about a task towards which an employee of yours shows motivation. Is his motivation a rational adaptation? What emotional reward is he getting out of it?

For example, John loves to work with Client A. They always make him feel valued.

2) Think about a task about which an employee of yours is demotivated. Could it be a rational adaptation? To which experience of his?

For example, John hates to send reminders. It is because when he does, the recipients do not care to reply or, when they do, they are angry. He feels rude for nothing. As a result, he stopped sending reminders unless his boss specifically orders so.

3) Is there anything you can do to provide him with an environment where the rational adaptation is motivation?

For example, John's manager committed to be more aware of what John is doing and to make sure that the good he does doesn't go unseen and unrewarded.

4) Set yourself a reminder on your phone or on your schedule to think, once a day for the following two weeks, about the following question. With my actions, which environment am I creating for my team, and what adaptations will it trigger?

CHAPTER 2
AVOID MOTIVATIONAL LOSSES

I clearly remember the day my actions caused a member of my organization to resign. It was during my first year in a management position. He handed his resignation because he expected a promotion that I didn't give him.

From my and my team's point of view, the decision not to give him the promotion was right and fair. Right, because he didn't deserve it. And fair, because other team members produced higher performance, and they earned the promotion more.

However, from his point of view, the decision was unfair. He often told me he expected the promotion, and I didn't make it clear enough that he was off-track. I didn't want to upset him. When someone got promoted instead of him, it came as a sincere surprise to him. The emotional shock was so big that he handed his resignation. (In the end, he did not quit. Even though neither of us work at that organization anymore, we are still good friends.)

The point is the following. **There is a difference between a decision being fair and it feeling fair** to the people involved. Employees are human. *Feeling* like they have been treated fairly is what matters to them. Bad managers just wish that their employees would be "more rational." Instead, good managers embrace the human nature of their employees. They take the required steps to make sure that their decisions are not only fair but also *feel* like that to everyone involved. How they do that is the topic of this chapter.

WHAT PEOPLE REMEMBER

J. F. Kennedy's "we choose to go to the Moon, not because it is easy, but because it is hard," and Martin Luther King's "I have a dream." Of great leaders, we remember their motivational speeches.

Some managers get the wrong lesson out of it. They believe that motivation is something that they can address through speeches. Their implicit assumption is that most workers are demotivated by default and require managerial action to gain motivation.

However, everyone who ever observed a kid knows that people are motivated by default. They are curious, engaged, and energetic. Then, at some point in their lives, the actions of their parents, teachers, or managers make them go through an experience teaching them the frustrating lesson that their efforts are not worth it. I call these experiences "motivational losses." Avoiding them is the key to a motivated team.

Avoiding motivational losses is more effective than attempting to instill motivation.

In fact, **motivation is like trust. It takes ages to build and moments to destroy.** Therefore, managers should direct most of their efforts toward avoiding motivational losses rather than towards engendering motivation.

(This concept complements the one seen in the last chapter – that motivation or lack thereof are rational adaptations to the environment people live in.)

MOTIVATIONAL LOSSES

Motivational losses usually arise from one of four causes.

- **Expecting a reward but not getting it.** This is the case of an employee that thinks he did a good job. He expects to receive at least a thank you. If he doesn't get any, he will learn the lesson that in his work environment, results aren't rewarded. He will adapt by losing motivation. (Crucially, what matters is not whether he *did* a good job, but whether he *thinks* he did. Hence why clarity is paramount in setting objectives, standards, and expectations.)

- **Expecting a reprimand but not getting it.** This is the case of an employee who thinks he failed his manager's expectations. He expects his manager to point out that his performance wasn't up to standard. He might not *want* it, but he *expects* it. If this doesn't happen, he will learn the lesson that in his work environment, low performance is okay. He will adapt by decreasing his future performance. (Again, what matters is not whether he *did* fail his manager's expectations, but whether he *thinks* he did. Hence why clarity is paramount in setting objectives, standards, and expectations.)

- **Expecting someone else to get rewarded or reprimanded, but it not happening.** This is the case of an employee who thinks that a team member of his did an excellent job (or a terrible one). He expects his manager to acknowledge or call out that. If it doesn't happen, the employee will learn the lesson that in his work environment, performance doesn't matter. He will adapt by lowering his efforts and caring less.

- **Expecting a project to evolve into something, and it not happening.** This is the case of an employee who works hard on a company initiative. Assuming he did everything on the to-do list, he expects the project to bring fruits. Perhaps, he expects his role in the project or in the company to grow in importance. If this doesn't happen (for example, the company "changed its priorities"), he will learn the lesson that in his work environment, it is not worth to spend time and energy on new initiatives.

The scenarios described above share two patterns. First, **employees expect their manager to appropriately acknowledge good performance and call out bad performance.** When this doesn't happen, they learn the lesson that in their work environment, it is not worth to pay the costs of high performance. The rational adaptation is to lower their efforts and sense of ownership.

Second, **employees adapt to what they think happened, not to what actually happened. Hence, you must set clear expectations that cannot be misunderstood. Then, you must be very specific in explaining why he awarded or reprimanded an employee.** Otherwise, you leave the door open to be misunderstood, even in good faith.

To prevent your team from experiencing motivational losses, you must set clear performance expectations and be consistent in following up on them.

MANAGING EXPECTATIONS IS NOT THE SOLUTION

Downplaying the expectations that performance is followed by consequences is not a solution. Yes, it will avoid motivational losses coming from expecting but not seeing them. However, it will also be the clearest statement that performance is not worth the effort. The result will be the same – your team will rationally adapt by reducing their contribution.

NOT A DECISION

Employees adapt to a work environment where performance is not rewarded by reducing their contribution. This is often not a deliberate decision. It is not a tit-for-tat. Instead, it is an automatic reaction – a form of conditioning. Do not blame your employees that react like that. Instead, provide them with an environment to which the rational adaptation is to increase one's contribution.

INFORMAL CONTRACTS

Every assignment you hand out to a subordinate of yours is an implicit contract. It stipulates that if the person to whom you are giving a task fulfills it, he or she gets an acknowledgment of his performance. If that implicit contract is broken, the result is a motivational loss.

The fact that there is no formal contract doesn't matter. Your subordinates perceive any responsibility assigned to them as a two-ways contract anyway. They expect positive consequences to good performance and negative consequences to bad performance. You are free to ignore this, but if you do, the consequence will be a demotivated team. Hardly a tradeoff you want to make.

I do not mean that you should reward your subordinates with a bonus for every task; a sincere thank you is enough. Nor I suggest that you must acknowledge every single task. For example, it is okay to set a weekly progress review. However, you must be explicit on the expected reward schedule. When is he expected to be evaluated for his work? By whom? What can he expect in case of a good job? And in case of a bad one?

The core idea is that **whenever you assign a task to a subordinate of yours, he will create an expectation of a reward in his mind. And unless you proactively clarify how and when it will happen, he will fill in these details for you.** If he does a job he believes to be good, and the reward does not come as per his expectation, he will lose some motivation. Perhaps not enough for it to be visible immediately, but he will lose some, and that can compound fast.

Assigning tasks creates expectations of accountability.

When unfulfilled, the result is a motivational loss.

IMPLICIT CONTRACTS AND THIRD PARTIES

If you assign a responsibility to someone and he fails to do a good job, you must call out his lack of performance. Not only to be fair to him, but to everyone else in your team too.

If you fail to call out a lack of performance, you create an environment that tolerates a lack of performance. The rational adaptation of all team members will be to reduce their contribution.

Whenever you assign a task or responsibility to an employee of yours, you create an informal contract that *everyone* expects you to respect – not just the person to whom you assigned the task, but all of his colleagues too.

ACKNOWLEDGING THOSE WHO MEET STANDARDS AND EXPECTATIONS

Whenever an employee thinks that his actions met your expectations, he automatically expects you to acknowledge him. He might not expect a formal reward, unless he greatly exceeded expectations or if there was a formal agreement in place, but he does expect some form of acknowledgment.[1]

It is your job to provide it to him – even if just in the form of a thank you, but it must be a sincere one.

You should acknowledge his performance even though it is not what you asked of him, as long as it is plausible for him to have misunderstood you. Thank him, then explain that you haven't been clear with what you expected*, take responsibility for that, make a commitment to be clearer in the future, and eventually delegate again the objective you intended to delegate in the first place. This reaction is much better than making him feel treated unfairly.

It's not about whose fault it was, but about what step forward has the best long-term impact on the team's morale, values, and performance.

(*): *This step is necessary in case any other teammate is witnessing the conversation. If you do not explain that you acknowledged performance you hadn't asked for because of a mistake from your side, the message that might pass to the rest of the team is "the manager rewards efforts, not results." Their rational adaptation would be to bring fewer results and to show more effort.*

---

[1] This is about day-to-day expectations. Of course, employees expect formal rewards, such as promotions or bonuses, in case of sustained performance over months, or in case of a personal success that produced a substantial profit for the company.

A CLARIFICATION

What matters is not the immediate effect of your actions on an employee's motivation, but their long-term effect on the motivation of the whole team.

Hence why, for example, choosing not to call out the bad performance of an employee of yours has a negative long-term effect on his motivation (his performance doesn't matter) and that of his colleagues (if there is no cost to bad performance, why should people put any effort?).

The above applies even in case some external problem caused the employee's bad performance – a family issue, for example. In that case, you should show understanding. It might even be appropriate to withhold any negative consequence. But you should always, no matter what, call out bad performance. Otherwise, you will run into the concerns described above: you will pass a message that bad performance is okay.

Analytically, your team members are smart enough to know that it was a special circumstance. But emotionally and unconsciously, they might still conclude that bad performance is okay. Hence the need for you to strive to be consistent with your actions.

MOTIVATIONAL LOSSES COME FROM MISALIGNMENT

We have seen how a misalignment between performance and consequences results in motivational losses.

The first of two possible sources of misalignment leading to motivational losses is the manager failing to acknowledge good performance and call out bad one. You can avoid this by being fair and consistent in dispensing rewards and punishments.

However, even if you get this right and correctly align individual outcomes with performance, it is still possible for employees to lose motivation. For example, your employees might disagree on whether a reward or punishment was deserved. This happens if they have a different idea of what constitutes good performance.

What matters from a motivation point of view is not whether the work environment is fair in rewarding results, but whether the people working there perceive it as such. **The second possible source of misalignment leading to motivational losses is the employee perceiving a different level of performance than the manager.**

Therefore, as a manager, **you must be clear both while setting expectations and acknowledging performance.** First, set clear and unambiguous goals and standards. Second, explain in detail why you are rewarding or calling out an employee of yours – both to him and, if appropriate, to the rest of the team. The clearer you are, the lower the possibilities of misinterpreting performance.

UNCOMFORTABLENESS INDICATES A LACK OF CLARITY

The first time I had to call out bad performance, I didn't. I was feeling too uncomfortable. I knew that my colleague's performance was inadequate, but I also knew that *he thought* that he completed his task well, and I did not want to break his morale.

We could have had different opinions on whether he completed the delegated task correctly because I hadn't been clear enough during the delegation. If instead I had taken the time to explain what I expected of my colleague, he would have known that what he did was not enough. **And because he would have known that his performance was inadequate, I would not have felt uneasy about calling him out.**

Uncomfortableness in calling out bad performance is a symptom of lack of clarity while setting performance expectations.

Taking the time to be unmistakably clear while setting expectations will make you feel less uncomfortable to call out those that failed them. You will find it easier, and you will do it more. The final result is that fewer people in your team will lose motivation from you giving a pass to bad performers.

ENSURING CLARITY DURING DELEGATION

It is best practice to ask the people to whom you delegate tasks to repeat what they understood their task to be. If, while they do so, you get any hint that they might have a different understanding of the task than you do, this is the time to tell them.

When the conversation ends, whatever the understanding that your team has of your expectations of them, it becomes an informal contract you sign with them – whether you agree or not.

It is worth spending some time early on to ensure that their understanding is correct.

ABOVE ALL, BE FAIR

Part of the art of management is seeing employees as people. They might be workers, but they are also human, and the latter determines their behavior more than the former.

For example, we saw that **managers must not only make fair decisions but also ensure that they feel fair to everyone involved.** If I had to summarize my managerial insights regarding motivation in a single line, it would be: **"above all, be fair."**

You might have noticed that you could have read this chapter and the previous one as if they had been written in a foreign language in which every word means "be fair." All the advice about giving your team members an environment where results are rewarded and bad performance is called out can be summarized as "create an environment where people are treated fairly (and feel like they're treated fairly)."

Of course, fairly does not mean benevolently. It means that there are known rules and that they are enforced to everyone equally.

First of all, it means that everyone knows what good performance is and that they trust that good things will happen to them if they achieve it. The same applies to bad performance. In a fair environment, everyone knows how bad performance looks. They expect their managers to call it out, every single time.

Therefore, to be fair concerning performance, you must take three steps. One, set objective criteria of how good and bad performance each look like. Two, make sure that everyone has the same understanding of these criteria. Three, acknowledge good performance and call out bad performance, every single time.

The first and second steps are necessary to make sure that you can perform the third one. Applying consequences to unclear performance metrics is unfair. Even if performance metrics are clear to you, and you are fair based on your appraisal of performance, it *feels* unfair. **The only way you can be fair, and be perceived as fair, is to take the time to ensure a shared understanding of what good and bad performance each look like.**

The above does not only apply to performance but to boundaries too. People expect you to tell them about boundaries in advance. For example, if there is a budget, tell them immediately. For an employee, it is terribly demotivating to hear at the end of the project, "you did a good job, but you overspent" or "you did a good job, but you could have used a larger budget." They feel unfair – you suddenly brought up a rule that you knew about, but they didn't. Hence why you should share all relevant information at the delegation stage.

That said, you cannot dump everything you know on your employees. It is confusing and might feel patronizing. How can you tell which information is relevant, then?

My rule of thumb is: "share whatever information you would feel upset if they ignored." For example, if you want something to be done in some way, and you would be upset if they did it otherwise, then you must tell them immediately. If you tell them later, or get upset later, it will feel unfair. It will break their motivation.

Hence, again, the role of fairness as a compass. From just the statement "be fair," you can derive the need for you to be clear during delegation, to create a shared understanding of performance standards and boundaries, to be consistent at acknowledging good performance and calling out bad one, and so on.

Most team management advice can be summarized in **"above all, be fair."** This simple advice is impossible to achieve without doing most things great managers do. Conversely, unfair managers, no matter how otherwise skilled, quickly hit a wall, for they will either find themselves with a demotivated team or a rogue one.

SOME MORE EXAMPLES

Giving a raise to someone who threatens to leave is unfair to others *and* leads the rest of the team to adapt by doing the same.

Increasing the workload of high performers is unfair and leads to everyone decreasing their contribution *unless* it is also paired with raises that restore fairness.

The two examples above demonstrate that asking yourself "am I fair" is a great way to gain awareness of the possible unintended consequences of your actions on the motivation of your team.

A SUMMARY OF THIS CHAPTER

- Your job as a manager concerning motivation is not to inspire but to prevent your team members from experiencing any motivational loss.

- Motivational losses are the rational adaptation to a work environment in which bad performance is accepted or good performance is unrewarded.

- You can prevent your team members from experiencing motivational losses by being unmistakably clear while setting expectations and by consistently acknowledging those that exceed them and calling out those that do not meet them.

- Above all, be fair.

EXERCISES

1) Think about a time that you lost motivation. What event caused it?

2) Think about a time that you caused someone else to lose motivation. Would more clarity have prevented that?

3) What can you do this week to prevent motivational losses in your team?

CHAPTER 3
SURFACE PROBLEMS

One of the hardest lessons I had to learn is that problems grow when ignored.

For example, I suffered for years of wrist pain due to poor posture while typing at my laptop. Denying the problem or taking painkillers prevented me from addressing the root cause, bad posture. My pain grew stronger. At last, I bought ergonomic equipment and forced myself to take more breaks. Only when I acknowledged the problem and addressed its root cause, it finally disappeared from my life.

Sometimes, problems go away by themselves. Most often, though, they grow and come back to haunt us, stronger and more painful.

Rule #003 of my book "100 Truths You Will Learn Too Late" says:

Problems grow the size they need for them to be acknowledged.

People who ignore this rule face larger and larger problems. Their lives are hard. Eventually, coping reactions such as avoidance or denial become their only option.

The problems they neglect grow more and more. The freedom that they were trying to hold onto by looking the other way gets destroyed anyway.

Conversely, people who proactively look for and address problems have easier lives and enjoy more freedom.

BAD MANAGERS VS. GOOD MANAGERS

Early in my career, there was this colleague of mine who, now and then, came late at internal meetings. It wasn't a big problem by itself, and his performance was otherwise excellent. So, my manager never addressed the topic. He thought it wasn't worth it. One day, my colleague showed up late at a customers' meeting. The customer was furious.

In hindsight, long-term problems are always worth solving.

...

Bad managers see problems as temporary inconveniences. Therefore, they ignore them or look for "band-aid solutions" – solutions that solve the symptom of the problem but not its root cause. The problems they hide or suppress keep growing. As a result, bad managers face larger and larger problems.[2]

Conversely, good managers see problems as indicators of something structurally wrong. They know that, eventually, they will have to address them. Better to do it immediately, before the problem causes irreparable damage.

Good managers address root causes even when the cost-benefit of doing so seems unfavorable. They understand that, today, basic cost-benefit analyses suggest the problems are smaller than the cost of addressing them. But they also know that unaddressed problems become more and more expensive to solve. Therefore, whenever good managers see indications of problems that are there to stay, they address them immediately.

When you decide whether it's worth addressing a problem, do not consider its current impact, but the one it might have if you let it grow stronger.

---

[2] The same applies to personal life. Health problems left ignored become more and more dangerous, and relationship problems hid under the rug become landmines.

SOLVING PROBLEMS BRINGS ANTIFRAGILITY

Even if problems didn't grow when left unaddressed, it would still be beneficial to make a priority out of surfacing and addressing them. The reason is a simple concept of paramount importance called *antifragility*.

The antifragile is what benefits from being under stress. For example, our muscles are antifragile: they get stronger when we use them (e.g., at the gym) and weaker when we do not use them. Conversely, a ceramic teacup is fragile: it stays strong when unused and gets damaged when we use it. Nassim Nicholas Taleb wrote an entire book on the topic, whose reading I recommend. What matters regarding management is the following.

Everything alive, including your muscles and including your team, is antifragile. It gets stronger under stress and decays when unused. This means that if your team never faces problems, it grows weak and complacent. Conversely, a team that regularly faces problems and addresses them grows strong and engaged.

Of course, facing too many large problems is bad, just as lifting too-heavy weights at the gym might tear a muscle. Too much stress causes burnouts and might damage the business. However, facing *no* problem is bad too. The key is to surface problems early so that you get a choice to address them while they are still small.

For example, video-streaming company Netflix achieves that by regularly crashing some of its servers at random. Not too many so that it would create an outage for all its customers, but not zero either. Netflix knows that by surfacing problems, it gets a chance to train its workforce and to spot structural problems before they are too big to create irreparable damage.

In the beginning, it is hard. Just like the first month at the gym is the hardest, solving problems feels hard and unnatural at first. If your team's problem-solving skills and mechanics are weak, you might want to start light. You can then progressively look for more problems as your team gets better at it – just like going to the gym makes you stronger and allows you to lift heavier weights.

> **Hiding problems makes your team weaker.**
> Surfacing them makes it stronger.

ZOMBIFICATION

Another reason for surfacing problems is that if you don't, your team will maladapt. **They will adapt to the absence of problems.** They will adapt by becoming complacent. They will keep doing what worked well before, even if it's not the best way to do things now, and even if it will lead to issues in the future. They will maladapt by playing politics instead of solving real problems. And they will maladapt by losing engagement and atrophying their brain, becoming zombies at work. You don't want that.

Of course, in theory, there are simpler and less painful ways to avoid zombification than surfacing problems – for example, trainings, team exercises, and conferences. In practice, these are nice-to-haves but do not avoid zombification by themselves. **The only sustainable way to avoid zombification is for your team to surface problems and address them.**

Growth also avoids zombification, but growth coupled with unsolved structural problems is a recipe for self-destruction – not a path you want to take carelessly.

TO TRIGGER ANTIFRAGILITY, PROBLEMS MUST BE SURFACED EARLY

So far, we have seen the following two points.

1) Problems grow in size when unaddressed. Hence, you want to surface them early, before they cause irreparable damage.

2) Teams maladapt when they do not face problems. Hence, you want to surface a lot of them.

Thankfully, the two points above go well with each other. Surfacing a lot of big problems might be too much for your team. However, **if you systematically surface problems early, you also ensure that you surface them small, so that they won't be too much for your team.**[3]

SURFACING PROBLEMS GIVES YOU TIME

The first reason people do not like to surface problems is that they like routine and dislike problems.

The second one is that people already have busy days. They do not want to add more tasks to them, even if their completion would be beneficial. However, unsolved problems take time away from us, more and more. For example, an employee lacking a critical skill will require help from the rest of the team, over and over. Conversely, training him takes time, but only once. Afterward, he will not need help anymore, and that will free time for the rest of the team.

In the long term, solving problems creates time.

It doesn't take it away from you.

---

[3] A fuller discussion of antifragility applied to the dynamics of organizations can be found in my technical paper "The Dynamics Of Risk-Taking", available on my website **Luca-Dellanna.com**

TOYOTA

Toyota production lines used to have a red rope hanging from the roof ("Andon Cord"). Workers of any level were instructed to pull on the rope every time they would notice a problem in the production process, such as a defect. Pulling on the rope would immediately stop production.

Everyone who ever worked in a plant knows how costly it is to stop production. And in Toyota, that would happen every time a worker – any worker! – would notice a problem and pull the red rope. What a great way to ensure that problems are solved immediately rather than being lost in a suggestion form!

Not only the red rope is a costly signal demonstrating that management is serious about surfacing problems, but it is also a wonderful way to align incentives towards solving them immediately.

To promote a culture of surfacing problems, use costly signals that the management believes that surfacing problems is worth its costs.

JUST IN TIME

In business school, many would describe Just In Time as the concept of having parts and components arriving directly at the production line the moment they are needed, to reduce the financial costs and handling time associated with having them delivered to a warehouse first. This definition is only partially correct.

It is true that renting space and having components handled twice (once to go from the delivery truck to the warehouse, and once from the warehouse to the production line) are two unnecessary costs that do not provide any value to the customer. However, cutting these two costs is not the only advantage of Just In Time.

Warehouses are buffers, and buffers protect against supply volatility. For example, if you have a warehouse with enough components, you can continue production even if the truck delivering components to your production line is late. At first glance, this seems good. However, it leads to zombification.

A company with a buffer (such as a warehouse with enough components to last a week) does not consider a truck being one day late as a problem. This means that no one in the company takes any step to ensure that the truck comes on time. If one day, eventually, the truck is one week late, production will have to stop, and the company will be unprepared on how to react.

Conversely, a company without a buffer (no large warehouse for components) will consider even a one-hour delay of the delivery truck as a problem. As a result, it will take immediate action to ensure that the truck comes on time, every time. As a consequence, its operations as a whole will become much more robust and efficient.

Buffers prevent problems from surfacing until it's too late. Instead, Just In time allows problems to surface so that they can be solved before it's too late.

Just In time is about removing buffers to surface problems.

Of course, not having buffers at all is undesirable too. It makes you fragile to sudden shocks, such as a supply line disruption. A possible alternative is to have the following attitude. **"Have buffers but make them hard to use." This way, in good times, problems are surfaced, and in bad times, buffers absorb them.** For example, you can have a stocked warehouse *and* rules that introduce friction to use it, such as requiring the signature of the operations manager. The harder the rule, the less your workers will use the buffer as a solution, and the more upstream problems they will surface and address.

A CULTURE OF SURFACING PROBLEMS

At my first company, I constantly surfaced problems. I loved doing it. Every time I did it, my manager always listened to me. That reinforced the behavior. If he ignored me, I would have lost my motivation fast.

For your team to surface problems early, you must first and foremost avoid that those who do it incur motivational losses. Moreover, you must provide an environment to which surfacing problems is the natural adaptation.

The learnings of the previous chapter apply here. Explain clearly and publicly that you expect your team to surface problems early. Then, consistently acknowledge those who do and call out those who don't. Finally, ensure that never ever an employee's reaction after he surfaced a problem is, "I should not have done it." A single motivational loss like that can be enough to undermine your efforts.

Your team will adopt a culture of surface problems if and only if that is the rational adaptation to the work environment you give them.

A note: of course, you want to avoid rewarding surfacing *any* problem to the point that your team members come up with made-up problems. You do that by defining very clearly what type of problems you are looking for, how they can and cannot be surfaced, and other boundaries. The next chapter will help you with this.

SURFACING PROBLEMS

Surfacing problems is not much about being skilled at spotting problems. Instead, it is about creating the right conditions so that your team members do not dismiss the problems they spot.

For example, I remember a client complaining that his line workers couldn't spot problems or come up with ideas to improve the existing processes. I was skeptical, because I knew that his company's workers were relatively expert. So, I asked him to show me. We walked to the production floor. He stopped a worker and asked him, "What could be improved?" The worker mumbled that he didn't know; everything was fine. Then, I asked him, "If you were the operations manager of the plant, what would you do to improve the process you work at?" He spent the next 8 minutes telling us his ideas for improvement, one over the other.

Most of your workers are already good enough at spotting problems. If they do not do it, it is because, at some point in their career, they have been taught that it's not worth doing it. Giving them the "authorization" to spot problems can be a game-changer.

CREATING AN ENVIRONMENT WHERE PROBLEMS ARE SURFACED

Often, you do not have to teach them new skills regarding problem-solving. **Instead, you must create an environment in which your team is empowered to surface problems, and good things happen to them when they do so.** My rule of thumb is the following. Do your team members already surface problems? If yes, it is valuable to teach them advanced problem-solving techniques so that they can spot problems that are currently invisible to them. If not, the problem is not that they cannot spot problems, but that they have been taught to ignore them. The solution is to explicitly say that you expect them to surface problems, to empower them so that when they do, problems get addressed (by them, or by some technical figure), and finally by taking costly action yourself to show them that you really mean it.

As an example, suggestion boxes are a terrible idea to get factory workers to surface problems or suggest improvements. What usually happens is that a worker uses them and expects an answer. Sadly, the boxes are collected only once a week or once a month. By the time someone reads the suggestion and takes action, the worker will already have learned that suggestion boxes are useless.

Instead, a manager keeping his office door always open (unless in a meeting) and taking the time to always listen to whoever walks in sends a costly signal that he does welcome suggestions indeed. As a bonus, it provides immediate feedback for the worker providing the suggestion without having to wait weeks as he would with a suggestion box.

Costly signaling and immediate feedback are great tools to build a culture of surfacing problems.

A PROCESS TO SURFACE PROBLEMS

Whatever process you set up for your workers to surface problems, it must:

- Provide fast feedback, demonstrating that surfacing problems is actually a desired behavior.

- Be costly for the company or the manager, signaling that, yes, we do want to hear from you.

- Ideally, provide regular cues or tools for workers to look for problems.

The third point is of lower importance, for it is effective only if you executed the first two points well.

Remember, it's all about the following question: are you providing your workers with an environment to which the rational adaptation is to surface problems the right way?

A SUMMARY OF THIS CHAPTER

- Problems grow the size they need for them to be acknowledged.

- Good managers proactively address root causes. They do so even when the cost-benefit of doing so seems unfavorable. They know that unaddressed problems grow larger and larger.

- Surfacing problems makes your team stronger. Hiding them makes it weaker.

- Without a culture of surfacing problems, teams maladapt.

EXERCISES

1) How much time do you and your team spend every week due to chronic problems? For example, due to a lack of good processes or skills, a lack of clarity, a problematic employee or customer, or something that should have been done but kept being procrastinated?

2) Choose one of the chronic problems identified in the step above. Then, schedule for tomorrow a time slot to address it. Do it even if your schedule is full – addressing problems once and for all is how you free time in your future schedules.

3) How are problems surfaced in your team? Who discovers them, how, how often, and what happens after they are discovered?

4) How could you put in place a system, process, and expectations to ensure that problems are surfaced often and early?

5) When a team member of yours raises the hand and says, "we have a problem," does your reaction make it more or less likely that he will surface problems again?

6) Is there any action you can take to make your team's environment one to which the rational adaptation is to surface problems and address them early?

CHAPTER 4
GIVE SPECIFIC FEEDBACK

If your kid comes to you with excellent results at the math test and you reward him with an ice-cream, what behavior are you rewarding (and reinforcing)?

If he studied, you rewarded studying. If he memorized the information, you rewarded memorization. And if he cheated, you rewarded cheating.

Generic feedback directed to a result without commenting on the behavior that achieved it can reinforce eventual undesired behaviors.

When giving feedback, be specific.

Otherwise, you might reinforce the wrong behavior.

BONUSES AND PROMOTIONS ARE GENERIC FORMS OF FEEDBACK

One of the reasons I dislike financial bonuses and promotions as the sole method to reward performance is that they are too broad. Their implicit message is, "do more of what you've been doing over the past few months, good and bad."

Bonuses and promotions are necessary to retain talent. However, they cannot be your only source of feedback. They might reinforce undesired behavior.

Instead, you want to compliment them with feedback that is specific and granular, handed out on a daily or weekly basis. You want to be able to talk to your employee when he does something good and say, "good job for this," and the next day, if you see him doing something he shouldn't do, walk to him and say, "you can do better."

The point is, **there must be a perfect alignment between what you say you want from your team and what you reward.** If you said you wanted performance, you should reward performance. If you said you wanted them to exhibit a specific behavior, you should reward specific behavior. And if you said you wanted performance and behavior, you should reward performance and behavior.

The sentence above means that **you should call out performance obtained with undesired behaviors.** Otherwise, you reinforce them.

Similarly, **you should call out desired behaviors that do not bring performance.** Otherwise, you will reinforce desired behaviors brought to the excess in which they're unrelated to performance – turning into undesired behaviors.

Calling out performance obtained with undesired behaviors might seem counterintuitive. After all, didn't you ask your workers to bring high performance? Didn't you ask them to practice the desired behaviors? **The key is to clearly explain that you asked them for both, and one alone is insufficient, no matter how well performed.** Just like a cappuccino with perfect foam but no coffee is bad, no matter how much you asked the bartender for a good foam.

GREAT COACHES

Gregg Popovich is perhaps the best basketball coach of our generation. Certainly, he is the one whose managerial style I admire the most. I remember having watched a game in which one of his star players made a 3-point shot. Usually, this is a cause of celebration. Instead, Popovich took his player out of the game. The reason? The shot was a bad one (it was taken in precarious equilibrium with a defender on his face – a shot that had slim chances to get in).

Coach Popovich understood that **feedback is about shaping behavior**. If he had celebrated the bad-yet-made three point-shot, he would have invited his players to take more bad shots. Instead, by benching the player who took the bad shot, he promoted the behavior he wanted his team to adopt – taking good shots.

There is a lot to unpack here. Let's see it bit by bit.

First of all, Coach Popovich understood that teams win games by taking good shots. In the short run, bad behavior[4] may bring a good outcome. With some luck, once in a while, a bad shot can score some points. In the long run, however, bad behaviors only bring bad outcomes. Hence the **focus on rewarding the behavior rather than the outcome.**

I do not mean that the score doesn't matter. After all, a coach is accountable for his team's performance. However, it is impossible to sustain a high score without having practiced the behaviors that sustainably produce a high score. Hence, in the day-to-day of great managers, their focus on the behaviors rather than on the score.

Measuring the outcome is important. But it must be subordinate to the behaviors that lead to it (as shown in the chart below). Otherwise, success is temporary or comes with hidden costs and unintended consequences.

---

[4] "Good" and "bad" behavior are respectively defined at what brings sustainable long-term results, and what doesn't.

	FAILURE	SUCCESS
DESIRED BEHAVIOR	**Comfort** (and reinforce the behavior)	**Celebrate** (and reinforce the behavior)
UNDESIRED BEHAVIOR	**Reprimand** (and show that the lack of desired behavior caused the negative outcome)	**Reprimand** (and explain that undeserved success cannot last)

In the chart above, the top-right and bottom-left quadrants are banal. Of course, you want to celebrate the desired behaviors that brought success, and you want to call out the undesired behaviors that brought failure.

The top-left quadrant is less intuitive. An employee that exhibits a desired behavior and then fails might learn the wrong lesson. He might conclude that the desired behavior does not lead to success, and therefore is not worth the effort. You want to avoid that. Hence the need to comfort your employees that fail after having practiced the desired behaviors. Thank them for the good they did. You might help them see that what they did was necessary but not sufficient to succeed. **Their failures do not mean that what they did wasn't good, but that there is something else that they should have done *on top of that*.** If possible, tell them personal examples of similar situations that you encountered in your career. Convince them that the desired behavior that they exhibited is still worth exhibiting. Explain that it is okay to make a mistake on the way to success (but not to keep making them). Choose your words carefully, to avoid them taking out the lesson that efforts are rewarded regardless of results.

The bottom-right quadrant is not intuitive either. You must call out those who achieved success through a behavior that has hidden or delayed negative effects – just like coach Popovich did with the player that took a bad shot. **It doesn't matter whether, that time, the shot succeeded. A team that keeps taking bad shots is bound to fail, eventually.** You want to explain this to your employee.

You should acknowledge his success. Dismissing it would make him defensive. It might even teach the wrong lesson that personal successes are ignored in your workplace. But you should also insist that his performance was unacceptable. Of course, a prerequisite to be able to do so without him feeling maltreated, is to have done the foundational work described in the previous chapters. Namely, you should have made clear that performance – in your team – is made of results, yes, but also of boundaries on what behaviors are unacceptable. Hence, **a good material result obtained through undesired behaviors is still a bad performance**, for it will lead to bad future outcomes. If that was made clear in advance, then your employees won't resent you when you call out their bad behaviors even though they brought results.

WHAT FEEDBACK IS FOR

Coach Popovich understood that **giving feedback is about how its audience will react to it.** That is the one lens that great managers always have in mind when providing feedback.

Feedback is about the reaction of the audience.

Good feedback is feedback that makes its audience react by expressing the behaviors that will lead to long-term success.

THE COSTLIER THE FEEDBACK, THE MORE EFFECTIVE

In the anecdote above, Coach Popovich benched one of his star players after he took a bad shot. It was a costly action – no one wants to risk upsetting one of his stars. But precisely **because it was a costly action, it sent a strong message.** It said, "in this team, bad behavior is punished, fairly, no matter who you are."

The costlier the feedback, the more effective it is.

Of course, Popovich could do so because, in the previous weeks, he took the time to explain the rules before enforcing them. He made clear that the team's objective was to take good shots, and that there would be consequences for those who consistently take bad ones. Because of that, when he benched his star player, no one was surprised. No player thought it was an unfair decision. Probably, not even the benched one. He might have been upset in the heat of the moment, but he probably knew it was a fair decision – hence, no resentment. Now, the team is more aligned. They internalized the lesson. Their future behavior became more supportive of the team's objectives. They got evidence that their work environment is fair and that their manager will follow his words with action.

The costlier the feedback, the more effective it is.

Your actions are a constant source of feedback, whether you intend it or not

FEEDBACK IS MADE OF ACTIONS, NOT OF WORDS

The old saying goes, "do not look at what people say, look at what they do."

Your employees know this saying very well. They adapt to your actions, not to your words. If you keep saying that you won't tolerate bad performance but your actions show otherwise, your employees will listen to what your actions say.

In the first chapter, we saw that teams are adaptive systems. Their members adapt to their work environment. Crucially, their work environment consists of actions, not words. They adapt to their manager's actions, not to his words. Or, to be more correct, they do in some measure adapt to his words, but when his actions contradict them, they forget about his words and adapt to his actions.

Rewards and reprimands, of any type, are considered actions. They are costly, and they impact behavior. Instead, cheap words, such as those pronounced in most meetings and announcements, do not impact behavior. Or they impact it, but only until his actions prove that they were empty words.

FEEDBACK MUST BE SPECIFIC

At the beginning of this chapter, we saw that generic feedback is bad because it might reinforce unwanted behaviors. For example, congratulating a salesperson on his numbers for the last quarter is good only if his high sales were genuine. Instead, if he sold a lot because he was offering excessive discounts, the congratulations will reinforce the bad habit of offering excessive discounts.

To avoid this risk, direct feedback to behaviors in addition to results. A manager congratulating his salesperson for having taken the time to understand his client's needs will reinforce the habit of understanding the client – usually, a positive behavior.

This does not mean that you shouldn't congratulate successes, but that you should do it only after having verified that they were achieved without any undesired behavior.

Of course, there is a chance that excessively reinforcing a desired behavior leads to the employee spending too much time on it, sacrificing other tasks. You can manage this risk in two ways. First, focus on reinforcing desired behaviors with little side-effects. These are behaviors that remain good even when they get excessively pursued. Second, be specific about the desired amount of the behavior, and then call out its excesses and side-effects. For example, you can say, "good job, Mark, for having spent the first half of the meeting understanding your client needs" and, if necessary, a few weeks later, "Mark, I appreciate that you're spending time understanding your client needs, but at some point, you should also move the sale forward."

GENERIC FEEDBACK IS DESTRUCTIVE, SPECIFIC ONE IS CONSTRUCTIVE

Generic feedback is destructive. If you give someone a generic comment such as "you're doing it badly," the chances are that he gets upset and stops listening to you. Not only generic feedback is not actionable, but it is also likely to provoke defensiveness at best and resentment or burnout at worst.

Conversely, specific feedback is actionable and more likely to be listened to. If you tell someone, "slide 14 is a bit too wordy, you might lose the reader there," they are likely to consider the comment. Specific feedback is more likely to generate change.

Generic feedback is destructive. Specific one is constructive.

That said, there is one more reason to use specific feedback, and it has to do with antifragility.

SPECIFIC FEEDBACK BRINGS ANTIFRAGILITY

In the previous chapter, I mentioned the concept of antifragility: the property of benefiting from problems. For example, our muscles benefit from being put under stress. Exercising makes them grow. Similarly, employees benefit from problems. A team that faces problems becomes engaged, develops skills, innovates, and improves its teamwork. Conversely, one that doesn't encounter problems grows complacent and obsolete.

Good feedback generates antifragility too. A worker who receives fast and relevant feedback becomes engaged, develops skills, and generally becomes better at what he does.

Just like problems, feedback generates antifragility only in the right amount. Too much, and people and processes break. But too little, and they decay.

The more specific the feedback, the more you can give without negative side effects. As we've seen in the previous page, specific feedback is more likely to be listened to and to impact behavior positively. Instead, generic one is likely to be ignored or to break the morale of the group.

Just like a key to antifragility was to surface problems proactively because doing so keeps them small and easier to handle, another one is to provide specific feedback. Doing so makes it more constructive and easier to handle.

Of course, common sense is a must. Making feedback specific makes it more effective and digestible. Even then, there is a limit to how much of it you can give to people. And of course, your attitude while giving it matters too. Practice will teach you the correct doses. But two things are certain. One, lack of feedback leads to decay. Two, when in doubt, make it more specific.

IF PEOPLE ARE NOT LISTENING TO YOUR FEEDBACK...

...the chances are that you're not specific enough, or that you're contradicting yourself.

The first point, specificity, was explained above. The second point, contradicting yourself, might occur if you only provide feedback when it's easy. For example, you might be providing your feedback on some employees but not on others to whom you might be uncomfortable talking. Alternatively, it might happen if you tell them that they should have done things in one way, but then you do them the other way, or give a pass to those that do it the other way. Consistency is paramount.

There are some instances in which it might be appropriate to give different feedback to different people regarding the same issue. It's okay to do so, as long as the reasons are made explicit, and they are coherent with previously set rules and boundaries. People are more understanding than most think when it comes to issues mentioned early and proactively, and less understanding of those mentioned late and reactively. As usual, above all, be fair.

A SUMMARY OF THIS CHAPTER

- **Generic feedback is destructive.** It is so broad that instead of targeting a behavior, it targets a person. Therefore, it is ineffective at producing the desired behavioral change. Instead, it is likely to trigger defensiveness or to reinforce the wrong behavior.

- **Specific feedback is constructive.** It is actionable, acceptable, adaptive, faster, prevents problems, and has fewer side effects than generic one.

- **The costlier the feedback, the more likely it is to change behavior.** Cheap feedback is more likely to cause problems down the road.

- **If you find that people do not listen to your feedback, you're not specific enough, or you're contradicting yourself.** Say it earlier, be more specific, talk in principles, never betray them, and people will listen.

EXERCISES

1) What is one piece of feedback a colleague, customer, teacher, or parent gave you that changed your behavior for the best? What was their attitude, tone, and choice of words?
2) What is one piece of feedback you received, which ruined the relationship between you and the person giving it? What was their attitude, tone, and choice of words?
3) Can you think of a piece of feedback you gave to a colleague of yours that he or she ignored?
4) Based on the learnings of this chapter, if you could go back in time, how would you reformulate that same piece of feedback?
5) When is the next opportunity for you to give specific feedback to one of your colleagues? (It must be within the next working day. Otherwise, you're not giving enough feedback. Perhaps, because you had bad experiences doing it in the past. Or maybe, because you do not spend enough time with your team. Anyway, strive to do it within the next day. It will make you a better manager.)

APPENDIX

There are two types of feedback: feedback regarding past performance and feedback regarding ideas. This chapter only considered the former. However, I wanted to add a few words regarding the latter.

In my book "100 Truths You Will Learn Too late," I wrote:

> The first way to kill an idea is by criticizing it. "It will never work."
>
> The second is by giving a suggestion. "Good idea, but here is how it could be better."
>
> Both drain the motivation out of the proponent. Many are motivated by being the ones bringing an idea to life, rather than by having their idea brought to life by someone else. Providing a suggestion that isn't critical deprives them of the prize of having been the ones solving the problem.
>
> Bestselling author Marshall Goldsmith formulated the 20% rule for providing feedback, which I would summarize as follows: "Unless you have a suggestion that brings at least a 20% improvement, shut up."

I love that rule. Following it will prevent you from stealing motivation out of your colleagues.

The 20% rule for providing feedback is an instance of the general Pareto rule – work on the 20% that produces 80% of the output.

The Pareto rule is usually presented as a prioritization method, but I would argue that it is a risk management method. Whenever you take an action, there are intended and unintended consequences. The intended ones are generally positive, and the unintended ones negative. It is much easier to predict the former than the latter. The implication is that, as a rule of thumb, you should favor taking actions with large enough positive intended consequences to offset the likely yet unknowable negative unintended ones.

For example, the obvious suggestion to prefer starting high-margin businesses is not only because, duh, they are more profitable. It is also because they have a higher margin of error.

Of course, the above is a very contextual rule of thumb and requires – as everything – lots of common sense.

CHAPTER 5
SYSTEMATICALLY REMOVE GREY AREAS

If you observed a typical marathon, you would discover that the single minute in which the most runners cross the finish line is 3 hours and 59 minutes.[5]

Runners optimize efforts to hit meaningful goals, and "running the marathon in under 4 hours" is one. This is why so many more runners cross the finish line at 3 hours and 59 minutes compared to 4 hours 1 minute and 4 hours 2 minutes.

In fact, if you plotted the number of runners crossing the finish line at any given minute, you would see three spikes: at 3 hours 59 minutes, 3 hours 29 minutes, and 2 hours 59 minutes. People tend to align effort and performance with meaningful thresholds.

This makes sense! Efforts are expensive. Increasing them makes sense only when there is a chance that they bring higher returns.

This relates to management. **At the workplace, there are usually two thresholds: good enough so that I get promoted, and good enough so that I don't get fired.** Many employees tend to calibrate their efforts so that they perform at one of these two thresholds.

---

[5] Plus or minus one minute, source: marastats.com

There are exceptions. Some internally motivated employees perform at a level between them. Those aiming at a promotion but still learning the skills to get there do the same. This chapter is not about them, but about that part of the workforce that has been long enough in their current role.

THE GREY AREA

In many companies, performance looks like depicted below. A green area where performance is up to standard. A red area where performance is so bad that you get reprimanded. And a grey area in between, in which performance is below standard but with no consequences.

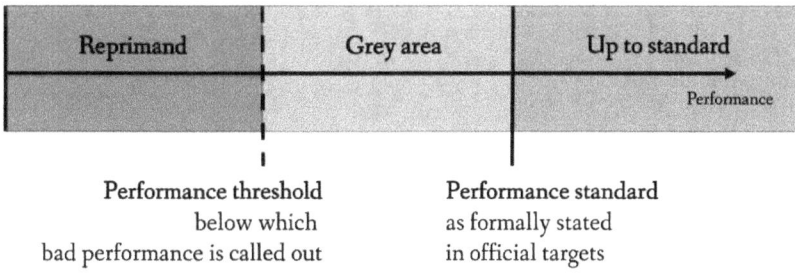

The result is that the performance of most workers hovers around one of the two thresholds. Internally motivated workers and those motivated by performance targets aim at the right threshold, the standard. Most other workers aim at the left threshold, the one below which they are reprimanded. Very few aim at any performance level in the grey area in between.

The lower the threshold below which bad performance is reprimanded, the lower the performance of everyone who doesn't aim at the performance standard.

Of course, there are exceptions to this rule. But in general, you will find that at least some of your employees adapt as described above, for at least some of the tasks you assigned to them.[6]

One implication is that the larger the grey area, and thus the larger the difference between the performance standard and the performance level bringing consequences, the lower will be the performance of the lowest motivated employees.

Therefore, **good companies strive to have no grey areas,** to raise the performance of their lowest motivated employees, as depicted below.

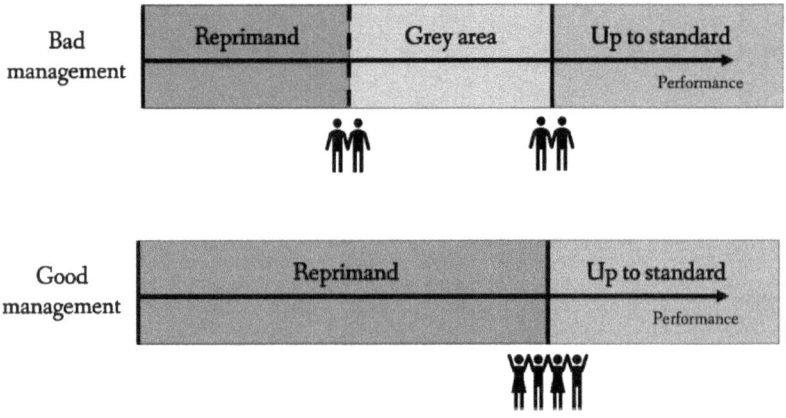

In great companies, there is no grey area. Performance is either up to standard or called out. As a result, most employees rise to the performance standard.

---

[6] Also, there are some second-order considerations to make, which are too technical to be included here, but can be found at **Luca-dellanna.com/fragilization**

Of course, only some tasks warrant the use of a "pass / no pass" performance standard, such as the one depicted above in red and green. Other tasks warrant the use of a performance scale with a few shades. For example, you might want to define what is good enough and what is so good that it warrants a bonus. This enables you to give your most ambitious employees a higher level of performance to aim for. The next page describes this case.

SHADES OF PERFORMANCE

The idea of removing grey areas does not mean that there can only be two areas, a red one and a green one. For example, there could be a third threshold above which performance is deemed excellent and worth special rewards such as bonuses, as depicted below. It is possible to have different shades of performance, but there should be no grey area between them.

The first chart depicted below represents a good example, and the second a bad one.

Reprimand	Up to standard	Worth a bonus
		Performance →

Reprimand		Up to standard		Worth a bonus
				Performance →

The second example is bad because grey areas are unfair. Employees performing above the standard required for a bonus expect to receive it. If there are grey areas, the company might decide not to hand them the bonus. They might argue that from their point of view, the performance wasn't good enough, or was good enough for a praise but not for a bonus. Either way, the employees incur a motivational loss, as shown below.

Please note that the above can happen even if the company, the management, and the employee are all in good faith and genuinely want to be fair. It's simply that, **the more the grey areas, the more the judgment of the people involved naturally differs.** And having different evaluations of the same situation is fertile growth for feelings of unfairness.

A SECOND EXAMPLE

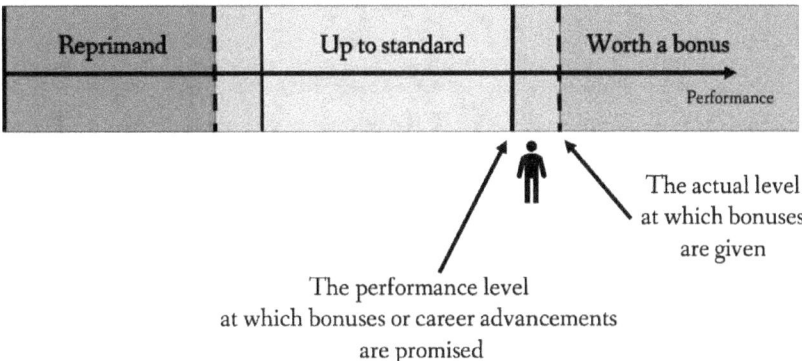

A similar situation occurs for a grey area between the red area in which performance is so bad that it is actually reprimanded and the green area in which performance is up to standard.

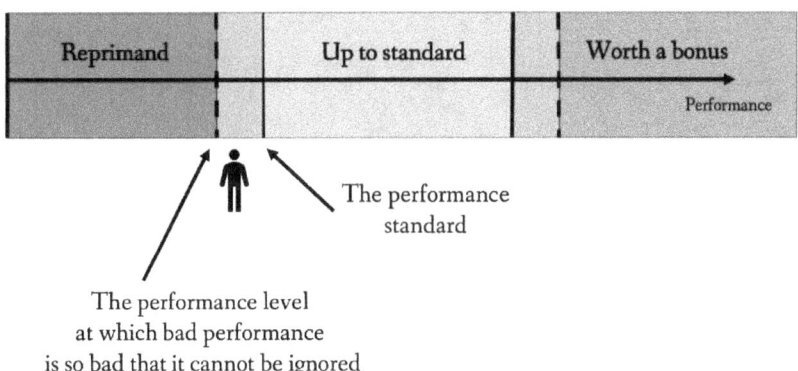

In the situation described above, if an employee's performance falls into the grey area, his colleagues performing above the standard expect the manager to reprimand him. If this doesn't happen, it feels unfair. They lose motivation.

Remember: it's not about whether it is unfair, but whether it feels so. The more the grey areas, the likelier that one party feels treated unfairly.

ABOVE ALL, BE FAIR

In Chapter 2, we saw the following principle. **"Above all, be fair."**

It is impossible to be fair with grey areas. The two examples above showed why.

A manager who strives to be fair will have to remove grey areas systematically.

A manager who attempts to be fair without removing grey areas is not fair but benevolent. And in a work setting, undeserved benevolence is unfair.

Of course, I'm not advocating for a dehumanizing workplace – the opposite. You can give some slack to great performers who make a mistake once. And you can give some slack to workers who have a sudden family problem. However, that slack should be explicitly motivated, and you should put boundaries around it. It's okay to clearly say that you lowered John's workload this month because his new baby doesn't make him sleep at night. It's okay to say that Mary shouldn't suffer large consequences for having made a single mistake after years of excellence.

However, it's not okay to quietly skip over John's bad performance. That would be unfair to his team members who might not know of his baby, or who could think that you're giving him slack because he's your favorite, or who might not know whether you'll also reduce their workload if and when they will have a baby. Grey areas are a source of motivational losses. Your job, as a manager, is to remove them systematically.

You can decide which performance standards to require, how to measure them, and when to relax them, but you must be publicly clear about that, and you must follow through with actions. Otherwise, you create grey areas.

Grey areas are unfair and dehumanizing.

STRIVE FOR NO GREY AREAS

Of course, in practice, it is impossible to have no grey area at all. But you should strive to have as few as possible, as little as possible. At any moment, every employee should know exactly whether the task he just completed is worth a praise or a reprimand. He shouldn't be guessing, nor should his answer be "neither." At most, he could say, "this part of my work was up to standard, and this one wasn't."

As a manager, you should ensure that all of your subordinates are always aware of what you think about their performance. At all times, they should know if they will be praised or reprimanded. For example, firing someone for bad performance without him expecting it is one of the strongest tells of bad management.

SOURCES OF GREY AREAS

Grey areas originate both during delegation time (the performance standard is unclear) and during performance evaluation (not all subpar performance leads to consequences and not all excellent performance is acknowledged). Hence the need, repeated over and over in this book, for managers to both set clear performance expectations and to apply consequences accordingly.

GREY AREAS ARE FERTILE GROUND FOR POLITICS

Some teams are plagued by politics: backstabbing and decisions taken with self-interest at mind. To get rid of politics, get rid of grey areas – only objective performance will be left.

DEMONSTRATING NO GREY AREAS

Removing grey areas will bring fast results **if and only if** you will have demonstrated a track record of consistently following your words with actions.

If your workers trust that you will call out their subpar performance, then removing the grey area between "good enough to be praised" and "bad enough to be reprimanded" will bring immediate results. Otherwise, workers will adapt their behavior only after you demonstrated that from now on, you do indeed call out any performance that is not up to standard.

Sometimes, the grey area is very large and/or some team members lack the skills to immediately perform up to standard. In these cases, you might want to aim for a progressive adjustment. For example, you can make the grey areas progressively smaller by raising the left threshold month by month. Or you could agree with your employees that you will train them, and that they have a few months to reach the required performance standard. Either way, remember the rule learned in the second chapter – above all, be fair.

IT ALL TIES TOGETHER

I love how everything descends from, "above all, be fair."

If you want to be fair, you cannot have grey areas.

If you want to remove grey areas, everyone must understand what your performance standard is.

For it to happen, you must set clear expectations, you must write them down (so that there is a document everyone can refer to), you must repeat them often, you must provide frequent feedback (to correct any misunderstanding), you must evaluate performance frequently (to ensure that no one is surprised with a bad year-end evaluation and feels treated unfairly), and many more actions that will make you a better manager.

A SUMMARY OF THIS CHAPTER

- Grey areas around what is unacceptable cause some employees to lower their performance below the acceptable.

- Grey areas around what is excellent cause motivational losses to those who perform excellently (or think so) and aren't rewarded appropriately.

- To remove grey areas, you must both set unmistakably clear expectations and reward performance accordingly – one is not enough.

- Above all, be fair.

EXERCISES

1) Did you ever experience a grey area in an objective set by a boss of yours?

2) How did you feel?

3) What could your boss have done to remove the grey area?

4) Can you think of any situation in your current role in which you gave or are giving your employees a grey area?

5) Is there any action you can take today to repristinate clarity and fairness?

CHAPTER 6
LEAD BY EXAMPLE WITH COSTLY SIGNALING

My book "Best Practices For Operational Excellence" begins with the following story of change.

At the crossroad of the 17th and the 18th century, a French chemist by the name of Éleuthère Irénée du Pont had to leave the country in a hurry. He had been a student of renowned chemist Lavoisier, but things recently changed. Due to political controversies following the French revolution, to escape jail and, perhaps, the guillotine, Du Pont took a boat and sailed to the New Continent.

On the 1st of January 1800, he landed in Delaware. Equipped with his chemical know-how, he began operating a gunpowder factory on the shores of the Brandywine River. As he would soon learn, gunpowder factories have an undesirable property: they tend to explode frequently.

Facing increased incidents, injuries, and deaths, he decided that he had to do something to reduce the explosions. How he solved the problem shaped the future of Operational Excellence.

Éleuthère du Pont took two initiatives[7]. First, he required that the Director (himself) lived inside the factory with his family. He put his life on the line. If something blew up, he and his family might die in the process – skin in the game.

Second, he established the rule that every new machinery had to be operated for the first time by members of top management. If the machine blew up, the manager would suffer the consequences on his own skin.

Needless to say, the safety of the plant increased overnight. Leadership demonstrated through visible costly actions is powerful.

The gunpowder company slowly grew into one of the largest industrial conglomerates in the world, DuPont. Its destiny would eventually cross mine two centuries later, as I would spend a few years working for its consulting business in Germany.

There is a lot to unpack in DuPont's origin story. Innovation, courage, skin in the game, and costly signaling. This last point is the topic of this chapter. In particular, we will see how costly signaling is the key to getting Core Values adopted.

---

[7] Also, there are some second-order considerations to make, which are too technical to be included here, but can be found at **Luca-dellanna.com/fragilization**

CORE VALUES ARE HARD

Many companies have Core Values such as safety, ethics, sustainability, customer-focus, respect for people, cost-savings, and so on.

Unless the Core Value originated right from the founder, such as safety in DuPont's example, managers find them very hard to introduce them in their organization.

Safety means that workers have to wear protective equipment that is expensive and slows their movements. Ethics means foregoing attractive opportunities. Sustainability means higher sourcing costs. **The reason Core Values are hard is that they represent short-term costs.**

Of course, Core Values also have long-term benefits. Safety means less downtime. Ethics makes recruitment easier and lowers legal costs. Sustainability brings brand power and institutional goodwill.

The long-term benefits of Core Values are higher than their short-term costs. This makes them attractive investments – that's why companies push so hard for their adoption.

However, **workers do not trust that their manager will be okay with them incurring the short-term costs of Core Values.** From their perspective, yes, their manager mentioned that the company cares about ethics, but will he really be okay when he sees that they refused a client for ethical reasons?

If the manager only used cheap words to communicate his support for Core Values, his workers will only practice them when short-term profitable. As soon as Core Values imply a short-term cost, workers take the safe choice: not following them.

Hence the importance for managers to communicate the importance of Core Values with costly signaling: actions that speak louder than words.

COSTLY SIGNALING

Diamond rings are expensive because words are cheap. Anyone can tell a lady, "I love you." In fact, it is so cheap to say that merely pronouncing these words is a very weak signal of intent. Hence the need for courting gentleman to demonstrate their love in more difficult or expensive ways, such as romantic gestures and jewelry.

Costly signaling is the principle that people trust more preferences signaled expensively.

Its importance is evident in relationships and advertising, but less so in management. And yet, costly signaling is the key to get Core Values adopted.

A manager who says that safety is important *and* follows-up by spending his precious time on incident investigations passes a much stronger signal than one who delegates them. His team will actually believe that it's okay to spend a bit of production time investigating incidents and making sure that they don't repeat.

When I tell executives that they should spend some of their precious time personally taking actions that demonstrate that they care about Core Values, I get objections such as "I do not have the time." That's precisely the point! It's because your time is valuable that how you use it becomes a strong signal of what you value.

AN EXAMPLE OF COSTLY SIGNALING

A few years ago, one of my best friends participated in a corporate training in Geneva, Switzerland. Her colleagues and their boss' boss – the Director – arrived almost one hour late.

The reason was that the bus that arrived to shuttle them from the hotel and the headquarters didn't have seat belts. Safety was one of the core values of the company, so the Director sent the bus back and requested one with seat belts.

The apparent cost-benefit of that decision was horrible! He sacrificed the precious time of about 20 high-level employees to get seat belts for what would have been a short bus drive. And yet, the Director enthusiastically decided to pay the cost.

He knew that if he didn't, he would have signaled that Core Values are possibilities, to enact only when easy to do so. Instead, by practicing the Core Value even when hard, he demonstrated that Core Values are certainties. They are safe investments that always bring returns.

*Note: it might not be true that Core Values **always** bring returns. But assuming they do is a necessary ingredient for your workforce to practice them so that your organization can grab their returns most of the time.*

HOW *YOU* PRACTICE CORE VALUES WHEN IT'S HARD DETERMINES WHETHER YOUR EMPLOYEES FOLLOW THEM

Many managers swear that they care about openness. They say that they have an "open door" policy – their employees can walk into the manager's office and raise issues at any time.

Sadly, what happens too often, is that one day an employee walks into the office, and he's told by the manager that "now it's a bad moment." The employee learns the lesson that the open-door policy doesn't really exist. He adapts by becoming less open. (Remember: people adapt to actions, not words[8]).

Instead, the best way a manager can demonstrate an open-door policy is by never turning down someone walking into his office. Of course, this necessitates boundaries to work in practice. For example, reserving the right to close the door during important meetings and calls. Or, when someone walks in, beginning with "Today is a busy day, so I only have 5 minutes, but I'm listening to you. If we need more time, we can set up a follow-up."

The point is, once you announce something for your team, ensure that you can follow-up with your actions. Avoid any motivational losses that can occur from your team expecting a behavior from you and not getting it.

Once you announce a Core Value or a policy, you must follow up with it, even when it's costly for you to do so. That's how you demonstrate that you believe that the Core Value is always worth it. That's costly signaling at work.

---

[8] Or, they adapt to words, until actions disprove them. Then, they adapt to actions, foregoing the previous adaptation to words. A process often by the name of "disillusionment."

CULTURE IS CREATED BY VISIBLE COSTLY ACTIONS

Culture is not made of perks and terminology, but of time- and cost-expensive rituals that are conspicuously perceived as worth it.

Costly signaling is how you can build this conspicuous perception of Core Values being worth their cost.

DO NOT HIDE

Bad managers who did not internalize the importance of Core Values try to hide the costs of practicing them. They think that the lower the cost, the better. However, by hiding the cost of an action, they also hide its importance. They miss an opportunity to influence their subordinates positively.

Good managers are not shy about these costs. They make them visible. Not in a transactional way – e.g., "We paid $15 each for the new safety gloves, you guys better use them now." – but in a way that is humble yet transparent, e.g., "We paid $15 each for the new gloves, it's a lot, but we think this is well-spent money, because Safety is just that important."

The more visible the costs and the higher they are, the more they will demonstrate to the workers the importance of embracing Core Values.

Do not misread the above and think that artificially inflating costs is a good thing: it is not. If a pair of good-quality safety gloves cost $15, saying that they cost $30 to your subordinates or buying a more-expensive-yet-just-as-good pair will only pass the message that you are a poor purchaser. The point is not to overspend, but to be transparent with costs.

A FEW MORE EXAMPLES OF COSTLY SIGNALING

A16Z'S fines. Silicon Valley Venture Capital firm Andreessen Horowitz (A16Z) charges its employees $10 per minute if they're late at meetings with entrepreneurs (their "customers"). What a wonderful way to signal to everyone that not wasting time and caring about customers is a Core Value of the company!

Amazon's doors. During the first months of life of the retail giant, when cash was not abundant, CEO Jeff Bezos and the rest of the employees used to work on desks made of a wooden door horizontally placed over two stands. The practice of using doors as desks continued for several years, even as cash became more available. Why? So that, when a new employee would join the company and ask why he is supposed to work at a desk made with a door, his manager could reply something along the lines of "here at Amazon, we look for every possible way to keep costs low and offer our customers the best price." What a wonderful way to impress a Core Value in the memory of a newly hired employee!

In both examples above, notice how both companies see cost as an opportunity to communicate what truly matters.

Building a healthy work culture while trying to avoid costly choices is like going to the gym trying not to get tired. Pain is where growth happens.

CONSISTENCY

Excessively theatrical displays of costly signaling tend to backfire as insincere. Moreover, they cost a lot of time and energy. Their performers cannot do them every day. Therefore, they end up sacrificing consistency.

Consistency is so important. People do not remember the 99 times that you keep a promise, but the one time that you break it.

DON'T BE A WEED

In his fantastic book *Alchemy*, Rory Sutherland wrote, "flowers are weeds with a marketing budget."

Sadly, many companies operate like flowers externally and weeds internally. They spend millions of dollars and thousands of person-hours in advertising and events, but then watch every cent and second spent on the production floor. Of course, waste should be minimized, but internal communication is not a waste – especially not the communication of Core Values.

I will be honest: of the hundreds of companies I had the chance to observe, not one successfully established a positive organizational culture without using costly signaling.

This doesn't mean that you must spend money on communicating Core Values – management time is a costlier and thus stronger signal.

Instead, it means that once you decided the principles that you want to permeate your team, you must stand by them, even when it's not easy, especially when it's not easy. That's when the returns are the largest.

A SUMMARY OF THIS CHAPTER

- Core Values are hard to get adopted because they represent short-term costs.

- Managers can drive their adoption by taking visible costly actions that demonstrate (1) that they believe that the benefits of Core Values are worth their costs and that (2) Core Values have to always be practiced, even when apparently disadvantageous to do so.

- Core Values become adopted when managers practice them *all the time,* not merely most of the time.

EXERCISES

1) What Core Values do you and your company stand for?

2) Pick one. What are its short-term costs? And its long-term benefits?

3) Is there any situation in which you or your employees do not practice the Core Value because it is advantageous not to?

4) Is there any action you can take to prevent that situation from happening?[9]

5) If not, the next time the situation takes place, you should take a visible costly action. Let your team know that the right course of action is the one that stewards the Core Value. Tell them not to worry about the costs: you will hold them accountable based on whether they practice the Core Value, not on the costs of doing so.[10]

---

[9] This is *via negativa*, the idea that it's easier to remove the source of problems than to take actions that manage their consequences. This idea is explained in detail in Nassim Nicholas Taleb's *Antifragile*.

[10] Within reason, of course. For example, you can say you will always approve an extra expense to buy safety equipment but you might put some criteria on its choice – for example, is the most expensive item okay? Is there any purchasing procedure?

If there's any boundary, this is the perfect moment to introduce them.

APPENDIX: COSTLY SIGNALING AND FAIRNESS

In Chapter 2, we saw the importance of fairness. "Above all, be fair," I wrote.

Too often, companies use fair words and unfair actions.

We saw that one of the reasons for unfair actions is a lack of clarity. If people have different expectations due to unclear communication, it is impossible to satisfy them without at least one party feeling like he has been treated unfairly.

The second reason for unfair actions is that acting fairly is often expensive in terms of money, time, status, and emotions.

Hence the importance of a two-pronged approach, especially if you manage managers or supervisors:

1) Be as clear as possible, so that you reduce the number of potentially unfair situations.

2) Explicitly mention that you expect your team to act fairly, no matter its cost. Promise that you won't reprimand them for the costs of being fair, but you will reprimand them for being unfair.

Fairness is the result of proactive action. It's hard to be fair without building the foundations that allow it.

CHAPTER 7

WORK ON THE ROOT CAUSES FIRST

In my book "100 Truths You Will Learn Too Late", I tell the following story by Jack Kent. Once upon a time, there was a little boy called Billy who found in his bedroom a dragon the size of a cat. Billy's mother ignored it, because there is no such thing as a dragon. Day after day, the dragon kept growing, ignored. One day, it grew so much that, with its size, it wrecked Billy's house. Faced with a destroyed home, Billy's mother finally acknowledged the dragon. Finally, it started shrinking. At the end of the story, Billy's mother asked, "Why did the dragon grow so big?" Billy answered, "It just wanted to be noticed."

Problems grow the size they need for you to acknowledge them.

There are many reasons for which problems appear. However, there is a single one for which they grow: if you ignore them.

PROBLEMS THAT GROW OVER TIME

Lack of clarity is a common problem that grows over time. First, we are unclear because we lack the time to be clear. Then, we are unclear because we are scared to admit that our past unclarity caused inconvenience.

Lack of clarity is terrible for two reasons. First, it provides fertile ground for motivational losses (as we've seen in Chapter 2). Second, it makes you less likely to hold people accountable. You do not want your team to perceive you as unfair, so you won't risk telling them that they did something wrong if your ambiguity contributed even slightly.

Hence the importance of being as clear as possible even when it doesn't seem worth spending the time to do so – the costs of ambiguity will grow over time.

Another common problem that grows over time is the **lack of costly visible signals.** We have seen in Chapter 6 that they are a necessary tool to show that you and the company believe that Core Values are worth their costs. The less you perform costly signaling, the harder it will be to start, and the less effect will you achieve.

A third common problem that grows over time is the **lack of consistency.** If you "give a pass" once to someone, others might request a pass too. The more "passes" you give, the more likely you will be to give another pass to someone else to avoid him feeling treated unfairly.

Other problems that grow over time include:

- **Bad hiring practices.** The worse people you hire, the worst your culture will be, and the worse will be your future capacity to attract talent.

- **Bad management.** If it lasts too long, your better colleagues will leave. You will be left with a team of degrading quality, which will make it harder and harder to correct the problem.

- **Bad time management.** The worse you are at prioritizing and solving old problems, the less time and energy you will have to tackle new ones.

ACKNOWLEDGING PROBLEMS

Sometimes, we neglect a problem because doing otherwise would be a hit to our ego.

More often, though, we fail to acknowledge problems because we do not think they are worth our time and energy. This happens when we would benefit from addressing the problem, but do not think that the benefits of doing so would be worth the costs of doing so.

One issue is that **we assess the cost-benefit tradeoff based on the current size of the problem instead of the one it will inevitably reach if we keep ignoring it.**

Another issue is that the more we wait, the more the problem grows, and the more painful it becomes to address it. Consequently, we often abandon any hope and suboptimally adapt our lives to live with it, allowing it to burden our lives every day.

Think about all the problems of yours that you hid under a rug instead of facing them. Probably, a few of them self-resolved. But others grew so much that you either had to address them at great cost or you left them untouched and suffered from them every other day. Has it been worth it to ignore them?

The second issue with solving problems is that we often tell ourselves we do not have the time or money to solve them. This might very well be true, but if you allow them to keep growing, won't they further erode into your time and money?

FINDING THE TIME TO SOLVE PROBLEMS

Note: The next three pages of this chapter have been published in my previous book, "Best Practices For Operational Excellence." They are so important to be worth repeating here.

Acknowledging problems is only the first step towards solving them. Finding the time to do it is the second one. As a manager, you are likely haunted by days with too much to do and too little time.

For many managers, the reaction is working longer hours. This might be needed in case of exceptional deadlines, such as the last days before a product launch, but it is never a good idea when its application is too frequent – more than 6-8 weeks per year. Chronic overtime brings stress and jadedness, both of which increase the risk of mistakes and limit the professional growth of the manager.

I once overheard an executive saying that he could not promote that employee who was working long hours because, if he did, the employee would find himself with too many responsibilities to juggle. He would either have to increment his working hours to the point of burnout, or inevitably "let some ball drop" and underperform. (Imagine the shock if the employee learned that – he thought that working long hours would help his career!)

In companies with poor management, working overtime signals commitment. Conversely, in companies with good management, it signals structural problems such as the inability to prioritize effectively and get stuff done.

Let me be clear: working overtime is not always bad. In small doses, it is good. Instead, it is systematically working overtime which is bad. The former represents taking care of unusual spikes in workload, whereas the latter represents working overtime to take care of the usual workload – an indicator of a structural problem.

Being understaffed might be the temporary reason for a chronically high workload, but it is never a long-term reason. A good organization that finds itself understaffed due to the sudden leave of a few employees or due to a sudden increase in business would quickly react and hire the missing talent.

SOURCES OF PROBLEMS

Each problem has a root cause. For example, your subordinates might continuously ask you for questions on a class of matters because the topic is not clear to them.

If, when they ask you for advice, you answer their direct question without training them to answer by themselves, they will keep asking you the same questions, causing you to spend too much time on it.

In general, **root causes keep generating problems. If you only solve problems without addressing their root cause, the root cause will keep throwing problems at you. Solving the root cause is the only action that will stop the flow of problems.** Just like, in a sinking ship, throwing water overboard with a bucket will accomplish nothing at all until you close hole from which the water keeps flowing in.

Every person with time problems has a prioritization problem. They only work on their superficial problems, on the urgent, waiting for the "perfect day" to address the root causes of their constant flow of problems. Sadly, that day will never come.

The day their problems will end will be the day they decide to work on the root causes of their problems, despite the problems they are facing.

MANAGING THE URGENT

Every day, there is something urgent to do. It is hard to find some time to work on the important – addressing root causes.

However, the very important never looks urgent. Solving root causes will always appear less urgent than solving the problems they generated.

Good managers aren't fooled by urgency. They know that their job is to work on the very important even when it doesn't seem urgent, ignoring the urgent if they must.

Companies with a bad operational culture reward the managers who work on the urgent. Instead, **companies with a good operational culture reward those who work on the important. They do so by subordinating managers' results on the urgent to their results on the important.** This might seem counterintuitive, but for example, Toyota reportedly had a policy where a manager could not get a promotion unless, regardless of the personal results he achieved, he also completed some goals regarding the personal development of his subordinates (i.e., taking care of the root causes).

This does not mean that the urgent cannot be important. It means that what to work on should be chosen solely based on importance, disregarding urgency.

Later chapters of this book discuss policies and tools conducive to addressing root causes. For the moment, I invite you to just focus on the following principle: the only way to solve your problems is by addressing their root causes; solving the problems themselves without caring about their cause will instead generate more problems.

GETTING MORE TIME

It is possible that, to your eyes, each of your subordinates is a source of problems to solve. If you only work on the problems they bring to your attention, they will keep bringing new problems to your attention, with your availability as the only limit.

I can guarantee that, if you spend more time today to train them to solve their own problems by themselves, tomorrow you will have much more time available, as they will not depend on you anymore.

Instead, if today you are answering their questions waiting for the day they do not have questions to train them to solve their problems by themselves, know that day will never come.

Of course, today, you won't have the time to train all your subordinates on all matters. Probably, you won't even have the time to train a single employee on all his matters. However, you have the time to train one of your subordinates to solve one type of problem he might have raised to your attention. If you do that, tomorrow you will have a bit more time (because that subordinate will not generate any more problems of that kind). You can use the time you saved for training a second subordinate on another class of problems, saving you more time during the following days. If you keep doing that, day after day, after a few months, you'll soon find yourself with much more time at your disposal.

If your subordinates come too often to you with questions regarding the same topic which require context-based answers, consider having a subject matter expert. He is a senior employee knowledgeable on the matter who would be responsible for answering questions on that topic – freeing time for yourself to do your job.

Let me debunk a myth here: having someone else do tasks that are not part of your job description is not laziness. It is lazy to do them yourself because you do not want to do the emotional work of putting yourself in the conditions of doing the critical tasks for your role.

The same might apply to other problems you might have, coming from sources other than your subordinates. Perhaps, your customers, your boss, your peers, bureaucracy, and so on. For each problem that you repeatedly encounter in your life, acknowledge that there is a root cause that keeps throwing new instances of that problem to you. Then, work on solving that root cause ignoring the problems it is throwing at you. That's the only way to avoid having to face the same problems in the future.

Chronic problems are life's way to tell you to do something you didn't do yet.

A SUMMARY OF THIS CHAPTER

- Problems grow the size they need for you to acknowledge them.

- Usually, we assess cost-benefit tradeoffs based on the current size of problems instead of the one they will inevitably reach if we keep ignoring them.

- Companies with a good operational culture reward those who work on the important. They do so by subordinating managers' results on the urgent to their results on the important.

- Root causes keep generating problems. If you only solve problems without addressing their root cause, the root cause will keep throwing problems at you. Solving the root cause is the only action that will stop the flow of problems.

EXERCISES

1) If you keep spending your workdays like you've been doing recently, how will your team's operational culture look like in a couple of years? How will your work life look?

2) Think about the last time that you avoided addressing the root cause of a problem. You might either have neglected it or attempted a temporary solution. Did it do you any good?

3) What is one problem that is taking away time from you?

4) Take your calendar and schedule *now* a moment next week in which you will address your problem once and for all. If your schedule looks too busy, remember that it is because of problems such as this one that are consuming your time. **Solving these problems does not cost you time but gives you time.**

CHAPTER 8

USE TIGHT FEEDBACK LOOPS

In school, people learn mostly through reading, listening, and memorization. Instead, in adult life, people mostly learn and improve through feedback loops.[11]

When you have a task, you do something to advance or complete it, and you observe the outcome. If it is positive, you learn that you did well and can do more of it. If it is negative, you learned that you should do something different next time. This is a feedback loop.

Sadly, many organizations leave feedback loops to chance. Some have a structured process for infrequent ones (such as year-end evaluations), but not for frequent ones, which are way more effective. This chapter will teach you what makes for a good feedback loop and how to build one yourself.

---

[11] Kevin Kwok wrote some great articles about how companies use feedback loops.

EXAMPLES OF FEEDBACK LOOPS

Here are a few examples of feedback loops:

- One-on-one meetings with your subordinates.

- Sending your presentation for feedback to your boss, peer, or mentor.

- Setting milestones and moments to evaluate progress.

However, good feedback loops are also tight. They provide feedback within one week from when the action was performed. For example:

- *Weekly* one-on-ones.

- Sending *a draft* of your presentation for feedback.

- Setting *daily* objectives and evaluating progress at the end of the day.

GOOD FEEDBACK LOOPS ARE FAST

You want your organization's feedback loops to be fast for three reasons.

The first one is that **the faster the feedback loop, the more feedback your employees receive, and the more they learn.** Someone who receives feedback every week progresses faster than someone who only receives it once a month.

The second reason is that **the faster the feedback loop, the more likely it will result in motivation.** If you compliment someone right after he did a good job, he will be more likely to feel good about doing that, and he will be more likely to repeat it in the future. Instead, if you wait too long, he might think that he did the job for nothing. That will produce a motivational loss.

The third reason is that **the faster the feedback loop, the more likely it will reinforce the right behavior.** For example, if you tell someone that he performed well *this year*, you might reinforce a desired behavior, but you might also reward an undesired one, such as taking shortcuts. You are leaving to chance which of the behaviors he displayed during the year gets reinforced. Conversely, if you tell someone that he did a good job right after he did something good, you will reinforce that behavior, not something else.

THE NECESSITY FOR FEEDBACK LOOPS

Usually, when I reach this point in the explanation of feedback loops, I get the following question. "Luca, feedback loops are great, but I don't think we need them. We're learning just fine."

This is a fair question. The answer is that **if you don't deliberately set your own feedback loops, your team will be influenced by pre-existing ones whose effect can be detrimental to the organization.** For example, employees already receive feedback loops from their social groups (the instinct to fit in) and from their bodies (the instinct to conserve energy). Similarly, a bad manager or a bad client might reward undesired behaviors. These feedback loops might dissuade effort, promote superficiality, put partisanship over principles, or just teach that "it isn't worth it."

These feedback loops are there whether you want them or not. Hence the necessity for you to set up competing feedback loops that steer your team's skills and culture in the direction that is beneficial for your organization and, in the long run, for them too.

SOURCES OF FEEDBACK

You, as a manager, should be a constant source of frequent feedback for your team. But you shouldn't be the only one.

You and your team should also seek feedback from:

- **Your colleagues, your customers, and your suppliers.** You should teach your team to seek formal feedback in the form of questions, reviews, 360° feedback, and similar tools. Or you can teach them to look for feedback in each interaction: how did the customer react? Did he get defensive? Did he sign the contract? Did he call back? And so on.

- **Lagging indicators.** You should assign to your colleagues some objectives or KPIs (Key Performance Indicators) that they can use as a source of feedback. You should set them so that if they are progressing towards them, they are doing a good job, and that if they aren't, they're missing something.

- **Leading indicators.** In addition to lagging indicators (metrics that measure past performance), you should assign to your colleagues leading indicators. These are metrics that measure progress on the fundaments of success: skills, habits, and systems. For example, if you want your salespeople to sell more (a lagging indicator), you should improve their selling skills (a leading indicator). You can do that by giving them some objective that measures their progress at the skill – for example, the number of trainings followed, the number of coaching sessions attended, or the percentage of leads converted to customers.

Lagging indicators reward results. Leading ones ensure that those results are achieved the right way, so that lagging indicators reinforce the right behaviors.

- **Your tasks.** You should train your employees to see every task of theirs, even if performed solo, as a feedback source. For example, what should they look at, or look for, to receive feedback while performing a given task?

- **Yourself.** What should you look at, or look for, in your own actions and reactions to receive feedback about your tasks, skills, mental habits, or beliefs?

SETTING GOOD FEEDBACK LOOPS

Here are a few examples of practices that set up tight feedback loops.

- Weekly one-on-ones. As a manager, you should have a one-on-one with your reports at least once a week. It can be long or short, face-to-face, or online, but it should take place on a weekly basis. Anything longer than that, and feedback loops are too loose. Unless your employees are both internally motivated and self-learners, they *need* weekly feedback to reach and sustain a high level of performance and job satisfaction.

- Feedback tools. Dashboards and performance self-tracking can become additional sources of feedback loops. Conversely, "360° feedback" and similar tools, while useful, are too infrequent to be relied upon for feedback loops.

- Trainings. At some point, you will benefit a lot from training your employees on the benefits of feedback loops. Help them set their own, as most appropriate based on their role and personality.

Training doesn't have to be formal. During the next one-on-one, you can explain the concept of feedback loops and assist them in setting one. Make the point that you are giving them a tool to help them improve, not to control them. Ideally, you should tell them that you won't ask them for the feedback loop's data but expect them to improve on a key skill.

TEACH THEM TO GET THE RIGHT LESSON

It might have happened to you that you learned the wrong lesson from failure.

Sometimes, failure means that what we did was wrong. Other times, it means that what we did was right, but not enough. For example, if our client refuses our proposal, it doesn't necessarily mean that we wrote it badly. It might mean that it was well written, but we gave it to someone who doesn't have the authority to sign it.

A very common failure mode of feedback loops is the following.

1) You set up a feedback loop.

2) You take an action.

3) The feedback you receive is negative.

4) You conclude that the action was wrong – even though it was right and failure was due to another circumstance.

5) You end up learning the wrong lesson.

People fail for two reasons. One, they take a wrong action or commit a mistake. Two, they take the right action and believe it is sufficient for success, whereas it is necessary but not sufficient.

Whenever you receive negative feedback, do not hastily conclude that what you did was wrong. Consider the possibility that what you did was right, but not enough.

You must teach this lesson to your team. Negative feedback or lack of progress do not necessarily mean that what they've been doing so far is bad. Perhaps what they did is good, and they just forgot one missing ingredient. Further analysis is required.

Teach your team that feedback loops are a starting point, not an ending one. Show them that they are a necessary part of improvement, though not a sufficient one. And explain that the fact that they aren't sufficient doesn't mean that they aren't necessary.

METAPRACTICE

In my book "100 Truths You Will Learn Too Late", I introduced the concept of metapractice in the context of sports, arts, and crafts.

> People who achieve mastery do two things differently: they practice more and adjust their practice more frequently. During each session, not only do they try to improve their skills, but they also try to improve their practice.
>
> Metapractice – the ability to tweak one's practice to maximize its effectiveness – is probably the most underrated skill of them all. After all, if one is bad at metapractice, he will find it difficult to learn any other skill.
>
> Do not just practice your skill – practice your practice.

The same applies to work. You should not only ensure that you and your team get tight feedback loops about your work-related tasks. **You should also ensure that you and your team receive tight feedback loops about such feedback loops.**

YOUR ORGANIZATION, BUT ALSO YOURSELF

This chapter mostly focused on how to set up tight feedback loops in your organization. Most of its contents also apply to how to set them up for yourself.

The better feedback loops you set up for yourself, the better feedback loops you will be able to set up for others.

Setting tight feedback loops across your organization requires time, skills, energy, trust, and confidence. You might or might not have them. But **if you set up tight feedback loops for yourself, you *will* eventually gather all the resources you need to properly set them up for the rest of your team.**

Begin with yourself first, and then teach to others.

A SUMMARY OF THIS CHAPTER

- The faster the feedback loop, the more feedback your employees receive, and the more they learn, the more likely it will result in motivation, and the more likely it will reinforce the right behavior.

- If you don't deliberately set your own feedback loops, your team will be influenced by pre-existing ones whose effect can be detrimental to the organization.

- Some sources of feedback: your colleagues, your customers, your suppliers, lagging indicators, leading indicators, your tasks, yourself. Also, use weekly meetings and dedicated feedback processes.

- Whenever you receive negative feedback, do not hastily conclude that what you did was wrong. Consider the possibility that what you did was right, but not enough.

- Metapractice: ensure that you and your team receive tight feedback loops about feedback loops.

- Of you set up tight feedback loops for yourself, you *will* eventually gather all the resources you need to properly set them up for the rest of your team.

EXERCISES

1) First of all, let's set up a feedback loop for yourself. Take a skill, habit, or task at which you want to become better. Is there any way you can receive feedback every time you practice it? Can you get feedback from someone? From something (data, recording, etc.)? From yourself (writing down notes, replaying it in your head, etc.)?

2) Second, let's set up a metapractice feedback loop for yourself. Take your calendar or to-do app and set-up a weekly reminder asking the two following questions: did you get enough feedback? How can you improve the quality and/or quantity of your feedback?

Remember: answers could be about being more consistent with your practice or about gathering more and better feedback – both help.

3) Third, let's set up a feedback loop for your team. Repeat the first exercise, but for a skill, habit, or task that you want your team to get better at. How can you set-up a feedback loop that will inform them on whether they're doing it right and/or getting better at it?

4) Fourth, let's set up a metapractice feedback loop for your team. Take your calendar or to-do app and set-up a weekly reminder asking the two following questions: did your team get enough feedback? How can you improve the quality and/or quantity of the feedback they receive?

5) Fifth: remove negative feedback loops. Is there any undesired feedback loop that is steering you or your team away from the behaviors that will lead to long-term success? What can you do to remove or delay it?

CHAPTER 9
GO WHERE THE WORK TAKES PLACE

If a manager does not know what goes on in his operations, he will not manage them properly. If his subordinates do not see him spending time where operations take place, they will not trust that he can manage them properly. For these two reasons, managers must spend time where the work they manage takes place.

There is no such thing as a leader who spends all his time in his office or conference rooms. Distance dilutes information and communication. Some things can only be learned in person, and some messages can only be delivered through personal action.

Senior leaders know that – they meet customers and shareholders in person, because that's what sends the strongest signal. A pity that many of them don't hold themselves to the same standard with regards to their own employees.

THE REAL PLACE

Toyota uses the term *Genchi Genbutsu,* the Japanese for "real place," to refer to "the place where the real work takes place." That's where managers must spend a considerable amount of their time. A CEO of a manufacturing company is supposed to spend time on the work floor, a sales team executive on the road with his subordinates, and a CEO of a retail company at his shops.

It is not just about gathering information first-hand nor just about learning. It's about communication. Senior leaders are busy and their time precious. That's why spending their time on the work floor sends such a strong signal – just like diamonds are a strong signal of engagement precisely because they're expensive.

If a CEO asks his employees to behave in a certain way, they might not follow, especially if the requested behavior is new or uncomfortable. But if the CEO displays the very behavior in front of their eyes, they will follow.

Of course, this sounds idealistic. But I assure you, it works in practice – if you are consistent enough and use the best practice described in the second half of this chapter.

LEVERAGE

On the previous page, I said that the CEO should spend time where operations take place. I was deadly serious. In my experience, CEOs and COOs of companies with great operational culture spend *at least* one hour a month on the work floor. (Operations Managers spend at least one hour a week, and lower-level managers much more.)

The larger the company, the more important it is to leverage the CEO's time. Hence, when he visits the work floor, he shall be accompanied by a few high-ranking or local managers. They will then replicate what the CEO did at their own subordinate's workplace. This way, the CEO's actions will have a rippling effect on the company.

Of course, the same could be done in a conference room, *in theory*. The CEO could meet with the top operations managers and set some objectives on the desired behaviors that the employees should display. These would then trickle down the hierarchical line until everyone in the company adopts them. This system is more efficient but less effective. In the real world, behaviors don't trickle down in conference rooms – and if it seems so, it is just because the CEO ratified behaviors that are already part of the company's DNA.

In real life, **operational culture changes with people walking where the work takes place and doing the work the way that they want it to become standard. The more important the person and the fewer its time, the largest the influence.**

My favorite best practice for managers to spend time where the work takes place is management walks. They are regular instances in which a manager takes the time to physically walk where his subordinates spend their time. Other Operational Excellence systems have similar practices called "Gemba Walks", "Line Walks," or "Observations."

WHAT HAPPENS DURING A MANAGEMENT WALK?

During a management walk, the manager performs the following set of steps:

1) He walks near where the workers are working and silently observes them. He takes care of following all required procedures (e.g., safety procedures such as wearing a helmet) to set a good example and convey the message that no one is exempt from following them.

2) He tries to catch something good, something bad, or something he does not understand. "Good" and "bad" refer to having followed the company's rules and Core Values.

3) If the manager notices something good, he personally thanks the worker for having done it.

4) If he sees something he doesn't understand, he asks the nearest worker for explanations. He is careful to adopt a posture of humility and openness. He avoids making any suggestions before having fully understood why things are done the way they are.

5) If he notices something bad, he walks to the worker who is working in a way that breaks the procedures, rules, or Core Values of the company. He politely interrupts him when it is safe to do so and asks him why he is acting the way he is. Perhaps there is a good explanation. A good manager doesn't assume that he knows better than his employees, unless he ascertained so. If there is indeed a good explanation for the behavior breaking the rules and procedures, then the rules and procedures must be rewritten to accommodate the circumstance. Otherwise, the behavior cannot be excused. The manager proceeds to remind the employee of the proper way of working and asks him to comply **with action** immediately. This way, he can verify correct understanding and allow a physical habit to form in the subordinate's mind. Finally, the manager thanks the worker for his time and collaboration.

It is important that the manager doesn't let pass any behavior which violates rules, procedures, or Core Values. **Either the rule or procedure must be rewritten, or the worker has to acknowledge he shouldn't have acted that way.** There is no grey area in between, no one-off exception. Letting an exception pass once is how exceptions become the new norm. Good managers never allow that.

Begin with openness to the possibility that the rule is wrong but, once you ascertained that it is not, be categorically inflexible in its application.

In case the worker had a good reason to act the way he did, and the rule or procedure has to be rewritten, the act of immediately ordering the rule or procedure to be rewritten is a Visible Action that shows that exceptions cannot exist. Either the rule or procedure is always right, or it is wrong. No such thing as "a procedure to follow most of the times" should be allowed.

WHAT TO LOOK FOR DURING A WALK?

There are two categories of situations to look for during a Walk: conditions and behaviors. Some drops of oil on the floor are an unsafe condition, whereas a worker walking on the shop floor without safety shoes is an unsafe behavior. Similarly, a poorly maintained machine is an unsafe condition, whereas a worker using a tool the wrong way is a bad behavior.

Bad managers only call out bad conditions and behaviors: situations that are unsafe or otherwise wrong, according to rules, procedures, standards, and Core Values. Instead, during Management Walks, good managers call out both good and bad conditions and behaviors.

Here is a non-exhaustive list of common conditions to look for: are there tools out of place? Are the walkways encumbered? Is any object placed where it could fall easily? Are the shelves messy? Is the space dirty? Is there any non-labeled machine or button? Is there any unlabeled container?

And here is a non-exhaustive list of common behaviors to look for: are the workers breaking safety procedures? Are they doing things the right way? Are they doing them the wrong way? Are they rushing? Are they multitasking? Are they walking or standing where they are not supposed to? Are they observing their mobile phone when they're not supposed to? Are they using the wrong tools, or misusing the right ones?

LOOK FOR BOTH THE GOOD AND THE BAD

Behavioral theory suggests that positive reinforcement (praising or rewarding someone for a good behavior) is more effective towards forming habits than negative reinforcement (reprimanding or punishing).

This does not mean that you shouldn't use negative reinforcement used. For the sake of consistency, you can never supersede any violation of rules, procedures, standards, or Core Values.

To maximize effectiveness, you should use both positive and negative reinforcement. Good managers lookout for both the good and the bad, and act on both.

TALKING TO WORKERS

Once they see a good or bad condition or behavior, managers should immediately initiate an interaction with the relevant worker. Praises and reprimands are most effective when given instantly after observing the object of the remark. If an immediate interruption would compromise the worker's safety, managers should wait for the first moment in which it would be safe to interrupt.

If the manager observed a good or bad behavior, he interacts with the worker having performed it. If the manager observed a good or bad condition, he instead interacts with the closest employee to the location where the condition has been observed. Some examples:

- If the manager observes a sharp tool left on the floor on the walkway next to an unattended worktable, he interacts with the worker assigned to that table.
- If the manager observes a sharp tool left unattended on the floor on the side of the warehouse, he is to interact with the closest worker to the tool that he can see at that moment. Even if that worker is just "passing by" – it's important to demonstrate the concept that rules, standards, and Core Values are a shared responsibility. Keeping an eye open for them is everyone's responsibility. **Holding peers, subordinates, *and superiors* accountable for rules, standards, and Core Values is everyone's responsibility.**

Some more on the last line. People are responsible both for achieving results and stewarding Core Values. Whereas accountability for the former has to trickle down the hierarchical line (with the CEO setting the objectives for his direct subordinates and holding them accountable for the results; these subordinates setting the objectives for their own subordinates and holding them accountable for the results, and so on), values are everyone's responsibility and everyone can and should call out any other person violating them – including executives, and, in case the violation happened on the company's premises, including customers and contractors.

ALWAYS CRITICIZE BEHAVIORS, NEVER PEOPLE

When calling out something wrong, managers should always direct the feedback or the critique towards the behavior of an employee, never to the employee himself.

No one likes being criticized *as a person*. The reaction is likely to be anger, frustration, or defensiveness. These emotions lead to ignoring the feedback at best and to spreading demotivation amongst the team at worst.

Instead, people are generally open towards receiving feedback on their behavior, especially if they believe that the person providing the feedback took some time to understand their point of view.

That's why managers should always take a few seconds to observe the worker before initiating a discussion and why they should ask, "why were you doing that" before criticizing one of his behaviors. Asking before commenting will both provide the manager with valuable intelligence and will make the worker more likely to be open to feedback.

ASK QUESTIONS THE RIGHT WAY

Managers should never ask questions with arrogance. Doing so would only have negative consequences. Instead, managers should ask questions by giving the benefit of the doubt (perhaps there was a reason for the way the subordinate was behaving) but also being firm in refusing all excuses. In this context, **every reason that does not require a procedure to be rewritten immediately or a disciplinary action towards someone else is an excuse.**

The wording of questions is very important. For example, I've noticed that asking questions such as "what would you change here?" is often replied with silence or indifference. Instead, questions such as "if you were the line manager here, what would you change?" are usually answered with enthusiasm and intelligence.

When asking questions, give your subordinates the authority to answer them.

COMMUNICATING STANDARDS AND PRIORITIES

Management Walks, like the rest of performance management, are about communicating standards and priorities practically and unambiguously.

Managers should keep this in mind at all times, never compromising on standards and priorities, *especially* during a Management Walk. That's when the managers' actions and priorities are the most visible.

MANAGEMENT WALKS ARE OPPORTUNITIES TO TAKE VISIBLE ACTIONS

Never break any rule or Core Value – in general, but especially while performing a management walk. Moreover, use management walks to show the desired behaviors you would like to become part of your organization's operational culture.

Remember Chapter 6, "Lead by example, taking visible costly actions." Management Walks are the perfect opportunity to do that. Make a point, during your Walk, to embody the highest standards of the operational culture you want others to follow.

If you don't, they won't follow.

Remember the point of this book: teams are adaptive systems. They adapt to the work environment they find themselves in. You are part of that environment. They adapt to you.

SCRIPT FOR A GOOD MANAGEMENT WALK

The manager walks on the factory floor. He looks left and right and sees a worker performing some maintenance on a machine without a helmet.

He spends a few seconds observing him. He then walks towards him, signals his intention of speaking with him, and waits for him to come. (Better not to interrupt him too abruptly, unless in case of imminent danger. Abrupt interruptions might result in sudden reactions or losses of concentration, which might themselves be dangerous.)

Manager: "Hi. Thank you for taking care of our machines." (Begin with a thank you, if possible. It should be genuine, related to an actual reason for saying thank you.)

Manager: "I've noticed that you aren't wearing the helmet. Is there any reason?" (Even if the rule is clear, the manager always tries to understand the worker's point of view, both to gather information and to make the worker more open to feedback.)

Worker: "Oh, sorry, it's just a two-minutes piece of work."

Manager: "Two minutes might be enough to injure yourself. Safety helmets must always be worn inside the factory. Your health is important." (The manager reinforces the concept that rules are never to be broken, and Core Values such as safety are never to be compromised.)

Manager: "Please wear a safety helmet on". (The manager asks the worker to comply immediately – not next time.)

Worker: "Okay."

The manager waits for the worker to take a helmet and wear it. (The manager shows that his words are always followed by action.)

The worker wears the helmet.

Manager: "Thank you for wearing the helmet. You're an important member of your team, and keeping you safe is in everyone's best interest." (Always thank the worker.)

Manager: "Is there anything else you'd like to discuss?" (Every interaction is an opportunity to gather intelligence.)

SECOND SCRIPT FOR A GOOD MANAGEMENT WALK

The manager walks on the factory floor. He looks left and right and sees a few machinery components on the floor, where they should not be.

He looks around and begins walking towards the closest worker, raising a hand to catch his attention. Then he says, "Hello. I've noticed that there are some components on the floor, blocking the walkway. Is there any reason?"

Worker: "John just left them there temporarily. He will pick them up as soon as he finishes his current task."

Manager: "I understand, but the walkway has to be fully accessible at all times." (The manager is inflexible and treats Core Values as priorities: never compromising on them.)

Manager: "Could you please put the components at their right place?"

Worker: "I will tell John to do that as soon as possible."

The manager looks around and sees that John is not in sight.

Manager: "Please do it yourself now, it's important. Safety is everyone's priority." (The manager does not risk that the worker forgets to tell John. The result would be that the components remain there for long, telling everyone that components can be left out of place. Moreover, the manager reinforces the idea of peer accountability.)

The worker reluctantly moves the components to where they belong.

The manager helps him or watches him. Either way, once the worker is done, the manager thanks him.

Manager: "Thank you for helping to keep the plant safe and the rules respected. They are here for a reason, and we should never compromise them." (The manager knows that the point of Management Walks is not only to spot what's being done wrong, but more importantly to reinforce the importance of procedures and Core Values with visible and costly actions – for example, spending a few minutes together with a worker to ensure that rules and procedures are respected.)

A SUMMARY OF THIS CHAPTER

- Distance dilutes information and communication. Some things can only be learned in person, and some messages can only be delivered through personal action.

- Operational culture changes with people walking where the work takes place and doing the work the way that they want it to become standard. The more important the person and the fewer its time, the largest the influence.

- Perform frequent management walks.

EXERCISES

1) Create a schedule for your Management Walks: book a 30-minutes slot in your calendar once a month if you are a member of Top Management, once a week if you are a manager, and once a day if you are a supervisor.

2) Perform the management walk, as per the contents of this chapter.

3) After you finish, take notes on what went right, what went wrong, and how to ensure that the next time you'll get more of the former and less of the latter.

4) If you are a manager or a member of Top Management, schedule a meeting with your subordinates in which you will ask them to implement Management Walks in their routine too. During the meeting, set unambiguous objectives on what constitutes a successful Management Walk and describe how you will evaluate them. I suggest that you accompany them during their first Management Walk, coaching them as they do it.

CHAPTER 10

TAKE DECISIONS NOT JUST FOR THEIR RESULT BUT FOR HOW THEY AFFECT FUTURE BEHAVIOR

The namesake principle of this book is that Teams Are Adaptive Systems. Their behavior is mostly an adaptation to their work environment. (Individual traits and personalities might affect how one reacts to a given environment, but that doesn't make the principle any less relevant.)

The implication is that **your major opportunity to influence your team's behavior is indirectly – by changing the work environment in which they operate.** They will then adapt to it. This gives us the following principle:

> As a manager, **take actions not for their immediate result but for how they will affect future behavior.**

For example, if a key employee of yours comes to you and says, "I found another job, give me a raise or I quit," it is tempting to give him or her a raise just to avoid the hassle and costs associated with finding and onboarding a worthy replacement. However, doing so would also pass the message that "raises are given to those who look for jobs outside." The next thing you know, your team will have adapted, and you'll find yourself under a deluge of ultimatums.

APPLICATIONS

Let's see how this principle applies to the previous chapters.

- Chapter 2. You should do everything you can to prevent motivational losses because employees adapt to them with lowered engagement.

- Chapter 3. You should surface problems because employees adapt to (manageable) problems with increased skills and motivation, and processes adapt to become more resistant. These indirect benefits are almost more important than the direct benefit of having solved the problem itself.

- Chapter 4. You should give feedback not only to correct a specific behavior but, most importantly, to show that you care and that standards are there to be met. Failing to do so will cause your team to adapt with disengagement.

- Chapter 5. You should systematically remove grey areas because teams adapt to them with lower standards and engagement.

- Chapter 6. You should lead by example with costly signaling, not for the direct effect of your actions, but for the behaviors that you will inspire and make possible.

- Chapter 7. You should prioritize working on the root causes not only because of the direct benefits of having solved a problem once and for all, but because if you do not, your team will adapt by pursuing busywork.

- Chapter 8. You should use tight feedback loops because they produce faster adaptation and lower the chance of maladaptation or undesired adaptation.

- Chapter 9. You should go where the work takes place, not because by doing so you learn more, but because your actions there will have a higher chance of influencing the behavior of your team.

I haven't yet seen a great manager who didn't act considering how his team will adapt.

FIRST- AND SECOND-ORDER EFFECTS

Any action of yours has direct effects. They are usually the reason you perform it. You assign tasks to get something done, or you give a raise to ensure that a good performer doesn't leave your team. Direct effects are also called first-order effects.

Most actions also have second-order effects. These are usually the result of how the system and its participants adapt to the first-order effects of your actions. In the previous example, giving a raise in response to an ultimatum keeps the employee (the first-order effect) and causes the rest of the team to learn that ultimatums are the way to get raises (the second-order effect).

This book's thesis is that **second-order effects dwarf first-order ones**, at least in the long term. Hence, you should make decisions based on the former, not (only) the latter.

THE TIME PROBLEM

"In the long term" is the key. There are two reasons we fall into the trap of taking actions that are first-order positive but second-order negative, and they both have to do with time.

If second-order effects manifested immediately, the first time we take a first-order positive second-order negative action, we would immediately see that the net effect is negative. We would learn our lesson, and from then on, we would optimize for the second-order effects. However, because second-order effects take days or months to manifest, we often fail to trace them back to the decision that caused them. Or we learn our lesson after assessing the short-term, before the long-term effects are evident. Either way, we overestimate the long-term impact of first-order effects and underestimate that of second-order ones.

The second problem with time is that we can only optimize for the long-term effects if the short-term ones wouldn't cause catastrophic consequences. For example, if the key employee of the previous example was working on an important project with an approaching deadline, refusing his ultimatum might be catastrophic.

Hence **the importance of working beforehand to avoid situations where you must take actions with negative second-order effects.**

THE WORK BEFOREHAND

When you are rushed, or your team is stretched, it is tempting to give in and take decisions that solve a short-term problem but introduce a long-term one. Sometimes, it might even be necessary, as in the example of a key employee working on an important project approaching a deadline.

Therefore, you must put in the work beforehand to avoid such situations. **You might not be in the condition of thinking about the long-term now, but it's your responsibility to get yourself in such a condition as soon as possible.**

Let's continue the previous example, in which a key performer came to you with an ultimatum, "a raise, or I quit." You might have made clear beforehand, with words *and* actions, that ultimatums are always refuted. Or, better, you might have appropriately rewarded your high performers financially and professionally so that they do not feel the need to look outside. And, just as a hedge, you might have built some hedges in the form of planned transitions or avoiding overstretching your team.

I know that it's easier said than done, but that doesn't make it any less true. Whenever you find yourself knowing that you should do something but cannot, take mental note of the obstacle. Then, when things are calmer, work to remove it so that the next time, it won't cause you to deviate from the right course.

And if things are never calmer, and you cannot seem to find the time to work on what would be good for your future and that of your team, ask yourself: if you keep doing things the way you're doing them, how will your life feel like in 10 years?

The way to go is the acknowledgment that nothing can be perfect, that there is no magic solution that will solve all problems, but that you can slowly but steadily achieve progress by meticulously addressing one root problem at a time and moving towards less and less actions that create a dysfunctional work environment to adapt to, and more and more actions that promote the right adaptations that will bring a sustainable future.

A SUMMARY OF THIS CHAPTER

- Your major opportunity to influence your team's behavior is indirectly – by changing the work environment in which they operate.

- Take actions not for their immediate result but for how they will affect future behavior.

- You must put the work beforehand to avoid situations where you must take actions with negative second-order effects.

EXERCISES

1) Pick an internal problem affecting your team – for example, a demotivated employee or a dysfunctional process.

2) Can you trace the problem back to someone adapting to his or her work environment? For example, is your employee demotivated because demotivation is the rational adaptation to his work environment? Or is the process inefficient because such inefficiency has advantageous side-effects for someone, given his or her work environment?

3) If so, what actions of yours (or of another manager) contributed to creating such a work environment?

4) Is there any action you can take now to change the work environment so that the rational adaptations to it are more conducive to sustainably producing great work?

CHAPTER 11
YOU ARE AN ADAPTIVE SYSTEM TOO

Everything in this book about team management applies to self-management too.

You are an adaptive system, just like your team. You rationally adapt to your work environment.

Yes, parts of who you are on the job are downstream of who you were before you began your career. But your work environment molded other parts of you – and will keep molding more in the future.

On the one hand, this phenomenon is a liability because there are parts of your work environment over which you have little control. Whether you like it or not, they will have some influence over who you become. On the other hand, it is an asset because you have at least some control over at least some parts of your work environment. You can leverage those to create adaptive forces that will shape you into someone more effective at achieving your goals (whatever your goals are – inside and outside of your company).

When direct change is too hard, try indirect one: change your environment to change yourself.

ACKNOWLEDGING THE INFLUENCE OF YOUR WORK ENVIRONMENT

Take a look at your schedule for today. How much of its contents were deliberate decisions of yours, and how much are the consequence of your manager or your company's structure?

Take a few seconds to remember the last internal meeting you attended. How much of the way it was run was a deliberate decision, and how much was it replicating the way meetings are run in your company? How much of the items on the agenda were deliberate decisions, and how much the result of what is generally discussed in similar meetings?

Take a Standard Operating Procedure and compare it with how you or your employees actually perform that task. How much of it depends on the text of the SOP document, and how much depends on how the procedure was run in the past?

Your work environment has a strong influence on what you do – often stronger than deliberate decisions. If you find yourself unable to make deliberate decisions or put them into practice, then you should work on changing your work environment. This includes your routines, schedule, physical environment, and relationships with your bosses, peers, and subordinates.

The following questions are good starting points:

- Which tasks of yours are not serving you or the company? (Common answers include obsolete tasks – tasks that were valuable but aren't anymore – and tasks solving a problem that does not exist.)

- Which meetings or procedures are rituals devoid of any utility?

- Which tasks, people, and locations are time sinks or energy sinks?

- Which instructions or processes are confusing?

- Which problems you're not learning from?

- What obstacles or bottlenecks are lowering your effectiveness?

THE PREVIOUS CHAPTERS, APPLIED TO YOURSELF

In Chapter 1, we saw that Teams Are Adaptive Systems. You are an adaptive system too.

In Chapter 2, we saw the importance of preventing motivational losses in your team, and how that could be done through clarity. Similarly, be clear with yourself and require clarity from others to avoid having to experience motivational losses.

In Chapter 3, we saw the importance of surfacing problems in the way your team and your organization operate. You should surface problems in the way you operate too.

In Chapter 4, we saw the importance of giving specific feedback to others. You should be very specific in your own feedback towards yourself too.

In Chapter 5, we saw the importance of removing grey areas. The plans and objectives you set for yourself should be without grey areas too. Moreover, you should also ask questions to remove grey areas from the plans and objectives others give you.

In Chapter 6, we saw the importance of leading with costly signaling. You should also lead yourself, especially when it's costly to do so. If you stay strong to your principles when it's uncomfortable to do so, you will solidify your principles and make yourself more likely to stick to them in the future.

In Chapter 7, we saw the importance of working on root causes first. Similarly, analyze your problems, obstacles, and weaknesses down to the root cause too.

In Chapter 8, we saw the importance of setting tight feedback loops for others. Set some for yourself too.

In Chapter 9, we saw the importance of observing the work where it takes place. Similarly, spend less time evaluating yourself based on the plans you make and more on the actions you take.

In Chapter 10, we saw the importance of taking actions not for their direct effect but for how they influence the future behavior of others. Similarly, take them for how they influence your future behavior.

SMALL CHANGES, BIG EFFECTS

The number one mistake people make when planning to change their environment is attempting too much. It might be daunting – and, let's face it, who has the time to spend on such a large change?

It is okay to plan a large change. But, if you do, set yourself a reminder one week in the future. If you will have taken no meaningful step by then, drastically reduce the scope of your plans, **no matter the reason you didn't take action.** I've seen enough to know that if action doesn't take place within one week, it won't ever.

Most people dramatically underestimate the impact of smalls changes. Yes, big changes are more impactful, but only assuming such big changes take place. In the real world, few have the time, energy, and skills to attempt big changes in one go. On the other hand, even a small change can have dramatic long-term effects, for it might free the space for a larger change to take place in the future. For example, if today you take 10 minutes to explain something to your employee that makes you lose 5 minutes a week, by the next month, you will have saved 20 minutes that can be put to use to something else.

A SUMMARY OF THIS CHAPTER

- You are an adaptive system, just like your team. You rationally adapt to your work environment.

- Your work environment has a strong influence on what you do – often stronger than deliberate decisions.

- If you find yourself unable to make deliberate decisions or put them into practice, then you should work on changing your work environment.

- It is okay to plan a large change. But, if you do, set yourself a reminder one week in the future. If you will have taken no meaningful step by then, drastically reduce the scope of your plans, no matter the reason you didn't take action.

EXERCISES

1) Go through the list on page 2 and write down any action points that come to your mind.

2) Do the same for the list on page 3.

3) Choose one item and commit to take action within the next week.

4) Set yourself a reminder for the end of next week, in which you will evaluate your progress on the previous task. If you completed it, great! Take a moment to appreciate how it made your work easier or more effective, and then commit to a new task from the list. If you failed to complete it, *no matter the reason,* write down a smaller version of it – something that would require half the effort. Then, commit to completing it.

CHAPTER 12
CHANGE IS ACHIEVED ONE FOCUS AT A TIME

Changing the way your team operates means changing habits and standards. Habits are what your employees do. Standards are the results they demand to themselves and to others.

To understand how to change habits and standards, we must first understand how we learn them.

HOW DO PEOPLE LEARN HABITS?

You probably never deliberately chose the sequence of actions you perform when you wake up, the way you chew, or the words you use to end your phone calls. **Most of your habits are the children of chance and repetition.** One day, for whatever reason, you did something in a given way. That made you more likely to do it the same way next time. A few more repetitions in, and eventually, it became a habit.

The same applies to your employees. Most of their habits result from them, one day, for whatever reason, doing things one way. And then doing it again the following day. And so on, until the habit formed.

Your goal becomes to avoid letting an employee performing a bad behavior twice in a row. Of course, it would be easier to avoid him performing it the first time, but that's impossible. You cannot train them on *everything* and expect them to do things as they were taught *every single time*. Instead, you must avoid the repetition of bad habits.

THE DANGER OF TWICE IN A ROW

It is human to err. Even your best employee might do something incorrectly once. Perhaps, on a very tiring day or while attempting to complete a tight deadline.

What happens afterward is paramount. Does he notice the mistake and corrects himself? Do you notice his mistake and correct him? If not, the first mistake opens the door to a second one, and a third, until it becomes a bad habit.

You want to have systems in place to catch incorrect behavior. Not for its one-time cost, but for the cost it would have were it to become a habit.

CATCHING INCORRECT BEHAVIOR

By "incorrect behavior," I intend here any behavior that deviates from your team's operating procedures and Core Values. It applies to both doing something forbidden or to not doing something required.

There are many systems to catch and correct incorrect behavior. The most common ones are checklists, audits, training, working in pairs, management walks, and simply spending time where your workers operate and keeping your eyes open.

Whatever the system, you must observe, communicate, and correct. It takes time, energy, and focus. You don't have them; not enough to keep an eye on everyone and every behavior of theirs.

You then have a choice. You can cast a wide net and catch what you can. But that means that even if you spot one incorrect behavior and you correct it, you won't be able to catch the next instance, nor all instances. You won't be able to avoid the deadly "twice in a row" that solidifies incorrect behavior into bad habits.

Or you can cast a tiny net that catches it all. Instead of focusing on all behaviors, you focus on one. Instead of focusing on all employees, you focus on one small team. This is the only solution in which you can be confident that you will be able to avoid the dreaded "twice in a row."

THE IMPORTANCE OF CRITICAL MASS

The other reason to prefer to focus on the adoption of a single behavior in a single small team at the time is that, if you don't, here's what's going to happen.

You tell *all* your workers to always wear the safety helmet while in the warehouse, *and* to keep the floor clean, *and* to re-organize the shelves in that corner. After your speech, they all grab a helmet and wear it – for one hour; then, it's lunch break. When they come back, one of them forgets his helmet. Because you're focusing on the corner shelves, you don't notice him. By the time you do, three other workers saw him working without the helmet and thought, "it's more comfortable, and nothing is happening to him. I should do the same."

Unless you enjoy playing whack-a-mole, the best way to create new habits is to focus on a single behavior in a small team and being obsessively consistent for a couple of weeks about it. Because you limited the scope of change, you can increase its consistency. You can make sure that for two weeks, every single time a team member will look at his teammates, he will only see them doing things the right way. You can ensure that for two weeks, no one will make the same mistake twice.

After a few weeks, the new habits will be so ingrained that you can move on to the next team or habit without the risk of losing the progress made.

Behavioral change requires critical mass. The only way to achieve it in practice is to reduce the scope of change.

A SUMMARY OF THIS CHAPTER

- Most of habits are the children of chance and repetition. To prevent the formation of bad habits, your goal becomes to avoid letting a bad behavior happen twice in a row.

- You want to have systems in place to catch incorrect behavior. Not for its one-time cost, but for the cost it would have were it to become a habit.

- Behavioral change requires critical mass. The only way to achieve it in practice is to reduce the scope of change.

EXERCISES

1) Pick one good habit that you would like your team to acquire (or one bad habit you would like them to lose).

2) Define the scope of change. Something such as, "this month, I will focus on getting team A to adopt behavior X." Keep it small: you want to be sure it's manageable.

3) Communicate to your team the behavior you want them to adopt. Be clear and explain why it's important. Use practical examples of what both desired and undesired behavior look like. Get them to promise commitment.

4) For the rest of the month, every time that you walk in the room(s) where the team operates, make a point of immediately checking whether anyone in sight is not complying. If so, remind them of the desired change. Otherwise, publicly thank everyone for respecting the procedures and Core Values (this will act as a reminder and show that you actually care about what you requested).

You should do this at least once a day.

5) Continue like this. If you do, change is bound to happen. If it doesn't, you probably haven't been able to spend enough time doing step (4). Restrict the scope of change and take action to ensure that you will be able to perform step (4) at least daily – for example, schedule a dedicated time slot in your calendar.

TYING IT ALL TOGETHER

In Chapter 1, we saw how **Teams Are Adaptive Systems**. Their members adapt rationally to what their environment rewards and to what it punishes. In Chapter 10, we saw the practical implication: **good managers take decisions not just for their result but also for how they affect their subordinates' future behavior**. And in Chapter 6, we saw an example: **good managers take visible costly actions to show that Core Values are trade-offs worth paying every single time**.

In Chapter 2, I explained that **you should avoid at all costs situations that can cause motivational losses**. In chapters 4, 5, 6, and 8, we saw how to do it: **give specific feedback, systematically remove grey areas, go where the work takes place, and use tight feedback loops**. The less time your team spends with an understanding of their current and desired performance that is different than yours, the more probable it will be that at some point, they'll face a huge motivational loss.

In Chapter 3, we saw the importance of **proactively surfacing problems**. Otherwise, teams adapt to the absence of problems – by making the company fragile or inventing their own problems, such as playing politics. And in Chapter 7, we saw the next step: **once a problem surfaces, don't mitigate its symptoms but address its root cause**.

In Chapter 12, I explained the necessity to **roll-out change step-by-step** by focusing on small teams at a time.

Finally, in Chapter 11, we saw that **everything written in this book applies not only to managing your team but to managing yourself too**. You are an adaptive system. Improve yourself by taking actions not for their immediate result, but for your behaviors that they make more likely.

ABOVE ALL, BE FAIR

When in doubt, use this principle as your guiding light: above all, be fair.

To follow it, you will have to be clear and upfront with problems. These are the qualities of good managers.

AFTERMATH

That was the end of the book! I'm glad you've read it all, and I hope you practices the proposed exercises.

If you enjoyed this book, please recommend this book to your friends and colleagues, or leave a review on Amazon / Gumroad / Goodreads.

In addition to my research and authorship work, I also do consulting on the topics of this book. If you want professional help in implementing the contents of this book or would like me to train your managers, do not hesitate to contact me at **Luca@luca-dellanna.com**

YOU CAN FIND ME ON…

I write regularly on Twitter (**@DellAnnaLuca**). My professional website and blog is **www.luca-dellanna.com**. You can contact me at **Luca@luca-dellanna.com** – I personally read all emails but appreciate conciseness.

At the end of this tome, you will find a brief overview of my other books.

ABOUT THE AUTHOR

An automotive engineer by training, after having led large teams and consulted for large multinationals, Luca quit his corporate job to become an independent researcher and author.

He dedicated his career to research the topic of emerging behavior and communicate its findings and their implications.

After having lived in Spain, Germany, Kazakhstan, and Singapore, Luca recently moved back to his hometown of Turin (Italy). He spends his days between consulting, teaching, and conducting his independent research from his home, a coffee bar, or a park.

Luca also consults corporations, startups, and individuals on behavioral change and antifragile operations. Once per year, he teaches a Risk Management module at Genoa University. He also regularly holds private workshops for entrepreneurs, operations managers, plant managers, and CEOs / COOs.

OTHER BOOKS BY LUCA DELLANNA

100 TRUTHS YOU WILL LEARN TOO LATE

"I am amazed at Luca Dellanna's ability to observe, compile, and articulate 99 very actionable life principles here. Each chapter describes the rule in a way that makes you think and then summarizes the action. It's filled with DEEP insights yet VERY readable."
– Theresia Tanzil

"Absolutely brilliant. You might have grasped some of these concepts before, but having them structured and in writing makes all the difference [...] I will surely recommend it to friends and co-workers."
– Alberto Pisanello

"A very thoughtful piece of writing, deep and wiring!"
– David Krejca

"Luca Dellanna's new book, "100 Truths," is super tight! [...] Practical, directional advice."
– Hari Meyyappan

"A thoughtfully written book in very straightforward language."
– A.L. Peevey

I wasted years of my life because I did not know its rules.

I did not know the rules of relationships, of careers, of health, of happiness.

Then, through hard work, talking with mentors, and trial and error, I uncovered some of them.

Now, I lay these rules out for you. In this book, you will find 100 of the lessons I learned.

It will still require hard work from your side to internalize them and put them into practice. Still, this book will make this process easier by letting you avoid committing the same mistakes I did.

THE CONTROL HEURISTIC, 2ND EDITION

"This book is like a magnificent suspension bridge, linking the science of the human brain to the practical craft of applying it in everyday life. I loved it." – Rory Sutherland

"A SUPERB book [...] by one of the profound thinkers in our field [behavioral economics]." – Michal G. Bartlett

"Luca's book was so helpful to my work. Opened my eyes up to some more reasons why change is so hard."
– Chris Murman on the first edition

At first look, human behavior appears as an inexplicable mess. Why do we behave irrationally? Why do *I* behave irrationally? Why is it so hard to change? What is happiness, and why does it seem to escape us?

We can only understand the brain as a distributed entity. The key to understanding it is to look at how the different brain regions interact with each other, how misunderstandings become illusions, and how selfish interests become irrational behaviors.

The Control Heuristic offers a new perspective to answer these questions. It provides a guiding light to shed the darkness of the subconscious resistances that prevent us from behaving like the man or woman we want to be.

ERGODICITY: DEFINITION, EXAMPLES, AND IMPLICATIONS, AS SIMPLE AS POSSIBLE

"Definitely worth reading! What I appreciate the most is that the author chose to explain the practical applications of ergodicity in layman terms, thereby making the topic accessible to a wide audience."
– Silvia Brumana

"Practical, easy-to-understand explanation of a complex issue. The examples the author uses make the definitions come to life"
– Scott Miller

"Very intellectually stimulating. It helped me think about risks at a deeper level."
– Tam HN

THE WORLD THROUGH A MAGNIFYING GLASS

"Thank you for helping me understand! My son was recently diagnosed, and I needed to be able to understand how he views the world. Why certain things would overwhelm him and cause so much anxiety and pain. This book made it so clear and easy to understand."
– Geiger T.

"Thanks to Luca Dellanna for his book about autism and ASD. It's probably one of the best works I have read in that matter (I have read a few), and it's surprising how realistically he depicts the condition."
– Manel Vilar

"Loved The World Through a Magnifying Glass – this analogy NAILS IT."
– Emerson Spartz, NYT Bestseller Author

This book is for parents, friends, or anyone related to someone with Autism.

This book is for neurologists and psychologists to help them understand the world of autism spectrum disorders.

This book is for people on the Spectrum, to help them understand themselves.

Some of the topics covered inside:

- The Magnifying Glass: a metaphor to understand perception under the Spectrum

- Why people on the Spectrum are impaired in contextual fields (such as personal communication) and advantaged in mastering detailed fields (such as computer science).

- Peripheral Functionality Blindness: the reason people on the Spectrum do not develop appropriate body language and facial expressivity.

- Prioritization by Specificity: the reason literal meaning is the only thing that matters for people on the Spectrum.

- The High-Pass filter: a novel hypothesis for the Autism Spectrum Disorder, coherent with previous theories and experimental results.

(Reading time is about 1h30)

THE POWER OF ADAPTATION

"This guy! Luca is amazing. So insightful with common-sense applications of complexity and the ability to communicate clearly!!" – Bob Klapetzky

This book is for you if:
- You like books dense with information.
- You appreciated books such as Taleb's *Antifragile*.
- You accept that the world is dynamic. Therefore, understanding how something changes is more important than understanding how something works now.
- You do not like usual business / self-help books that provide solutions that only work in the short-term.

"The Power of Adaptation" focuses on the topic of adaptation as the main force shaping the world as we know it. However, adaptation is an emergent process. Therefore, it cannot be understood through narratives, nor can it be acted upon directly. This book aims to describe the underlying phenomena which weave together into what we perceive as adaptation. It is a guide to practice **the four behaviors that will help them harness, rather than fight, change.**

BEST PRACTICES FOR OPERATIONAL EXCELLENCE

A book on Operations Management for CEOs, COOs, and Operations Managers.

Written by an author who understands complex systems and how to design antifragile operations.

Inside:

- The Four Principles of Operational Excellence.
- The Eight Best Practices of Operational Excellence.
- How to roll-out and sustain a change initiative.

ACKNOWLEDGMENTS

To my wife, Wenlin Tan, for the love and joy she brings to my life.

To my mother, for supporting and loving me all my life, and to Franco, for loving her. To my father, for the same and for stirring intellectual curiosity within me.

To my family in law, for having raised my love and having taken care of me while I was at their house.

To my friends and everyone else who, directly or indirectly, knowingly or unknowingly, contributed to my well-being.

To my Patrons Ross Screaton, Malcolm Ocean, Ricardo Ortiz Noguera, and Pablo Cárdenas. Their help gave me stability on top of which I could conduct my research.

www.ingramcontent.com/pod-product-compliance
Lightning Source LLC
Chambersburg PA
CBHW050004230526
45465CB00003BB/1250